A CAMERA CRUSADE

PLATE I.

A WOMAN OF SAMARIA

John iv. 7.   *There cometh a woman of Samaria to draw water.*

Isaiah liii. 7.
1 Cor. v. 7.
Heb. xi. 28.
Rev. v. 12.

PLATE I

A WOMAN OF SAMARIA

John iv, 7. There cometh a woman of Samaria to draw water.

John iv, 7, 9; ii, 13.
Ex. xii, 3–7, 13, 14.
Isaiah liii, 7.
I Cor. v, 7.
Heb. xi, 28.
Rev. v, 12.

A CAMERA CRUSADE

THROUGH THE HOLY LAND

BY

DWIGHT L. ELMENDORF

WITH ONE HUNDRED
PHOTOGRAPHIC ILLUSTRATIONS

NEW YORK
CHARLES SCRIBNER'S SONS
MCMXII

TO THE MEMORY
OF
MY MOTHER

FOREWORD

In 1093 Peter the Hermit returned from a pilgrimage to Jerusalem and gave such a pitiful account of the unhappy situation of the Christians in the East that he aroused all Christendom to such a degree that armies were raised and in 1096 started toward the Holy Land.

The wars carried on by the Christian nations of the West from the eleventh to the latter half of the thirteenth century for the conquest of Palestine were called Crusades, from the Portuguese word *cruzado*, that is, "marked with the cross," because the warriors who followed the holy banner wore the sign of the cross.

In 1901 I started for the Holy Land with my ever-faithful camera on my back, my only weapon, simply to journey through the land with a desire to see for myself places mentioned in the Bible, to study ancient customs which still remain, and if possible to understand the significance of many sentences in the Scriptures which were very obscure to me and to those who tried to teach me; in fact, my faith was wavering, I was in doubt, yet one verse in Matthew compelled me to go: "Ask, and it shall be given you; seek, and ye shall find; knock, and it shall be opened unto you."

I went, I asked, I knocked: I doubt no longer, now I know. The journey on horseback through the Holy Land was a revelation to me; may my description of it be a help to many.

DWIGHT L. ELMENDORF.

CONTENTS

ILLUSTRATIONS

ILLUSTRATIONS xiii

A CAMERA CRUSADE

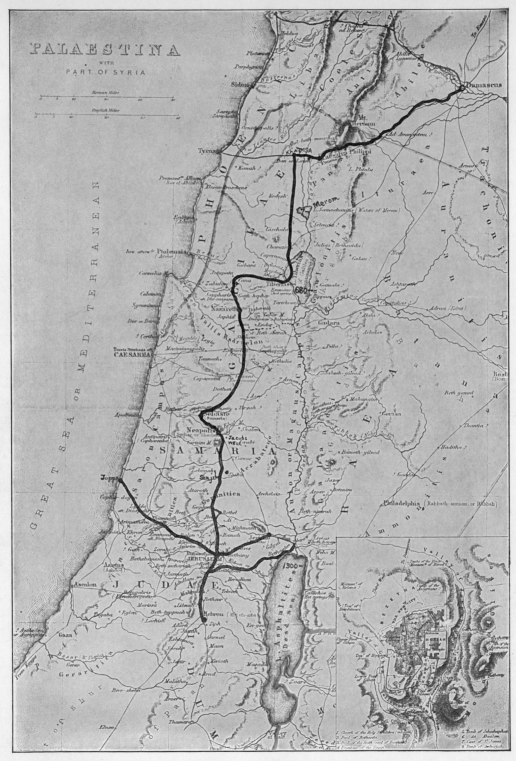

Map showing route followed by the author. It is indicated by the black line starting at Joppa

A CAMERA CRUSADE
THROUGH THE HOLY LAND

THE SOUTH

AFTER many days we arrived off the coast of Palestine and came to anchor near Joppa. What thoughts arose in our minds as we gazed upon that land for the first time; the Promised Land, that land that has been the great passageway from south to north and from east to west, the little land that has produced the three great living religions of the world, the Holy Land.

There being no harbor, it is necessary to land in small boats, and no landing at all is possible in rough weather.

One of the remarkable features of the whole coast line of Palestine is the utter lack of harbors. For this reason the land was never attacked by sea. Not long after our arrival quite a fleet of row-boats, propelled by motley crews, swarmed about our vessel in utter disorder, and we received our first impressions of the natives of the land of the present day; it seemed as though Bedlam was let loose. One must expect to find this state of things in every Turkish port; no discipline, no order, wild gesticulations, and loud, yelling voices unpleasant to the ear, impudent demands for tips or "bakshish," and generally rough treatment. Passing through the custom-house, we walked through a dirty street to a hotel.

After making all arrangements with a dragoman, or head guide, I wandered to the "house of one Simon, a tanner," climbed upon the roof, and there for the first time saw a real Oriental roof, made to live on as well as under.

In the centre of it was a square opening, large enough to let down "the bed wherein the sick of the palsy lay," which actually happened in Capernaum. (Mark ii, 4.)

From the roof there was a fine view of the rocky shore where the cedars of Lebanon were landed for the building of the temple at Jerusalem. Legend states that the prophet Jonah started on his remarkable voyage from one of these rocks, and near by are shown some bones of a gigantic sea animal.

Upon another rock are some chains with which (according to legend) Andromeda was bound till rescued from the sea monster by Perseus.

In the market-place were many interesting scenes of Oriental flavor, some of which indicated the abject condition of womanhood under Islam rule.

One handsome fellow in bright-colored costume was peddling Syrian bread, which looked good but tasted like very sour corn-bread spread over with ripe Roquefort cheese; it was awful, but after two weeks in the Holy Land I could eat things worse than that. This bread seemed to be typical of the condition of the land to-day, or rather of the Christian religion as evinced there to-day by many of the various church sects of which I shall speak again.

Joppa was anciently a Phœnician colony in the land of the Philistines. Now it has become an important place on account of the great number of pilgrims who arrive there every year. It is interesting to the traveller because of the pure Semitic types to be seen for the first time.

From Joppa lead three great roads, or highways; one to Nabulus (Shechem), another to Gaza, and the third to Jerusalem.

For quite a distance the Jerusalem road leads through the famous orange groves of Joppa into the plain of Sharon, the Hebrew name for the plain between Carmel and Joppa. In the early spring the ground is brilliant with the blossoms of the red anemone, the "Rose of Sharon."

One of the striking features of the plain is the tower of Ramleh, or the tower of Omayyad khalif Suleiman (A. D. 716), from the top of which is a charming view toward Lydda, which is mentioned in a very early period in connection with the legend of St. George. Mohammed declared that at the last day Christ would slay Antichrist at the gate of Lydda. This is simply a distorted version of the story of St. George and the dragon. The whole Maritime Plain presents a scene of quiet beauty, a marked contrast to the inhospitable coast which always was considered the western boundary, and the sea, a barrier instead of a highway. This plain, rising in gentle undulations toward the Shephelah, now so peaceful and fruitful, has ever been one of the most famous war-paths of the world, through which Thothmes, Rameses, Sennacherib, Cambyses, Alexander, Pompey, Titus, Saladin, Napoleon, and many other great generals have led their armies. Truly this Maritime Plain may be likened to a bridge between Asia and Africa. From their hills the Jews could watch all the spectacle of war between them and the sea years before Jerusalem herself was threatened.   (Isa. v, 26.)

Lydda, or Lod, was one of the most westerly settlements of the Jews after the exile, for there were no smiths in Israel; so the Hebrews came down to the Philistine border to get their ploughshares and mattocks sharpened. (I Sam. xiii, 19.)

From Ramleh we journeyed up through the vale of Ajalon (Josh. x, 12) toward Jerusalem, and turned south toward Hebron.   On the way we passed the valley of Eshcol, from which the spies sent out by Moses brought a cluster of grapes, and from the appearance of vines growing there to-day one might imagine they dated back to the time of Moses.

Near Hebron we camped under the shade of an ancient oak known as Abraham's Oak, in the plains of Mamre so closely connected with Abraham's life.

Hebron, a city older than Zoan, is now occupied by the most fanatical and detestable specimens of Mussulmans I have ever come in contact with.

Now no Christian dog is permitted to enter the mosque with two minarets, built over the double cavern of Machpelah, the burial-place purchased by Abraham from Ephron, the Hittite, when Sarah died. Isaac and Jacob are said to be buried here also. Of the many traditions which cling to the vicinity of Hebron, two are most interesting which localize the creation and the death of Adam here.

So many things actually happened at Hebron, or very near it, that one may entirely discard all legends and traditions and be satisfied with historical facts. After the many references to Abraham and his family, we find that the city was destroyed by Joshua and became the chief city of the tribe of Caleb. David spent a long time in this vicinity, and after Saul's death he ruled over Judah from Hebron for seven and a half years.

"When Abner was returned to Hebron, Joab took him aside in the gate to speak with him quietly, and smote him there under the fifth rib, that he died, for the blood of Asahel his brother."

And David caused the murderers of Ishbosheth, the son of Saul, to be hanged by the pool of Hebron.

During the Muslim period the town was still important not only on account of its commerce, but also as a sacred place, owing to its connection with Abraham, who was represented by Mohammed as a great prophet, and to this day the Arabs call it "El-Khalil," or the town of the "friend of God."

Being repelled in every way by the fanatical inhabitants, we were glad to leave the town and turn northward toward Bethlehem. On the way we passed the pools known as Solomon's Pools, the upper of which is best preserved. We camped on a hill overlooking the Shepherd's Village, where the shepherds "watched their flocks" just below Bethlehem, the place of bread, the city of David.

It was well that we did not enter Bethlehem that evening, for as twilight waned we sat on the ground like the shepherds of old and gazed toward that sacred spot where "she brought forth her first-born son, and wrapped him in swaddling-clothes, and laid him in a manger, because there was no room for them in the inn." "And they shall call his name Emmanuel, which being interpreted is, God with us;" "and he called his name JESUS."

Until very late we sat meditating, not speaking to one another, overwhelmed with the consciousness of being near the place where the most momentous prophecy was fulfilled.

The next morning I stood before the low, narrow entrance to the Church of the Nativity, or the Church of St. Mary, perhaps the oldest Christian church in the world, and wondered why the great doorways had been walled up with heavy masonry. I soon learned that this was done to prevent the Mohammedan soldiers from driving their horses into the church and using it as a stable.

The exterior of the church is in appearance very ancient and not at all imposing. The interior, divided into three parts, one belonging to the Greeks, another to the Latins, and the third to the Armenians, is a great surprise and is very impressive. The church is built over the traditional birthplace of Jesus Christ. In the crypt is the manger, entirely different from those depicted by great painters, and yet, with all the lamps and decorations removed, it is exactly like many a manger I saw in actual use in the land.

Not one of the paintings of the Nativity that I have seen gives the slightest idea of a Syrian manger. Perhaps that by Murillo, in Berlin, or "The Holy Night," by Correggio, in Dresden, are the most beautiful, though not correct.

Whether this traditional manger is the exact spot where the Saviour was born matters little to me. If this is not the place, it must have been very near by; far above this little matter of doubt is the great fact, "Fear not: for, behold, I bring you tidings of great joy." . . . "For unto us a child is born, unto us a son is given: and the government shall be upon his shoulders: and his name shall be called Wonderful, Counsellor, the Mighty God, the Everlasting Father, the Prince of Peace."

It is of more than passing interest to note that the "Bread of Life" was born in Bethlehem, which in Hebrew means the place of bread.

From the most ancient times this region in the immediate vicinity of Bethlehem has presented a marked contrast to the surrounding wilderness, for that is what most of Judea is. Around the town are many fertile fields apparently fenced in by stone walls, but these are simply formed by the stones picked out of the fields themselves. The finest are the "Fields of Boaz," just below the city toward the Dead Sea. Here is the scene of the beautiful idyl of Ruth. Even to this day the gleaners follow the reapers who often "let fall also some of the handfuls," for the method of reaping has not changed since the time of Moses. After the reaping comes the threshing, which is done on the old-fashioned threshing-floor.

As we journeyed from Bethlehem toward the Dead Sea, I saw two shepherds leading their flocks into green pastures. This was such a beautiful illustration of the Twenty-third Psalm that I talked with the shepherds and asked one of them to go around to the other side of the hill and then call his sheep. He did so, giving a peculiar call—"Br-Br-Br-Br—Ha-Ha-Ha-Ha!!!" Instantly the sheep looked up, began to bleat, and ran toward him—they knew his voice. Then I tried to imitate the shepherd; the sheep looked up, but they would not follow; they ran from me. "And a stranger will they not follow, but will flee from him: for they know not the voice of strangers."

Hanging from the arm of one of the shepherds was a curious leathern bag made from the whole skin of a kid. In it were several round stones and a sling made of camel's hair. When a sheep wanders too far away the shepherd puts a stone in the sling and casts it cleverly so that it strikes the ground directly in front of the wandering sheep, causing it to look up and so notice that it has gone astray—"All we like sheep have gone astray: we have turned every one to his own way."

This took me back to the time of David (I Sam. xvii, 40): "And he took his staff in his hand, and chose him five smooth stones out of the brook and put them in a shepherd's bag which he had, even in a scrip; and his sling was in his hand: and he drew near the Philistine." This seemed to me but as yesterday, for I was living amid customs that have not changed in thousands of years. Is He not "the same yester-day, and to-day, and forever"?

When a shepherd goes out alone he invariably carries with him his pipes, made of reeds, upon which he plays the weirdest melodies. Strange as it may seem, this music keeps the shepherd from becoming crazed by solitude.

After leaving the shepherds we began to penetrate the wilderness in earnest. Palestine is not an easy land to journey through on account of the many valleys, or wadys. One of the deepest and almost impossible to cross is the valley of the brook Kidron which flows down from Jerusalem to the Dead

Sea. In a remote part of this valley is situated the monastery of Mar Saba belonging to Greek priests. In the fifth century a settlement of monks was founded here by St. Euthuymius. His pupil Sabas became famous for his sanctity and founded the order of Sabaites; hence the name.

As we approached the region near the Dead Sea the wilderness became still more desolate, and this desolation extends from the Dead Sea up to within an hour or two of Hebron, Bethlehem, and Jerusalem; so that it is easy to realize the effect upon the ancient natives of Judea, judging by that upon the casual visitor—an overpowering sense of how narrow the border line is between life and death, a realization of the power of the Almighty who can make contiguous regions so opposite in character. The prophets Amos and Jeremiah both felt the fascination of the desert and painted many a word picture of the wrath of God or of his divine grace.

The story of Saul's hunt after David and the latter's narrow escapes becomes very vivid to one traversing these valleys, all alike, where large parties of men might encamp near each other without being aware of it. In addition to this wilderness being a refuge for fugitives, we must remember that it was where John the Baptist was prepared for his mission, and it was here that our Lord suffered his temptation.

All the way from Bethlehem the route seemed to be descending until we caught a glimpse of the Dead Sea far below us; then we realized that we were approaching that remarkable sink thirteen hundred feet below the level of the Mediterranean Sea and thirty-eight hundred feet below the altitude of Bethlehem.

Although it was March, we began to suffer from the intense heat. Still we wound our way around barren hills until we stood on the shore of the Dead Sea, the water of which is so heavily impregnated with salt and other chemicals that no fish can live in it. So dense is this water that it is almost impossible to swim in it; the body floats on the surface as if it were cork.

As we gazed in every direction through the peculiar haze ever present in this part of the Jordan Valley, we saw no signs of life; everywhere evidences of death and destruction. Of the cities that once thrived in this awful hollow, not a trace is left. Though Sodom and Gomorrah were destroyed centuries ago, the glare of that catastrophe is still terrible in the symbolism used by the prophets and our Lord.

From the place where the river Jordan flows into the Dead Sea, it takes about an hour to ride to the Jordan ford. Pilgrims are attracted to this spot because of its association with John the Baptist and the baptism of Christ.

The Jordan, as a river, was a great disappointment to me, for it is not even picturesque. The water is turbid and warm and hardly fit to drink on account of its salinity. The banks are covered with a rank growth of reeds, thorn bushes, and stunted trees which plainly show the effects of the spring freshets, and the current is very swift, rushing along as if enraged at being compelled to flow into the Salt Sea.

From the Sea or Lake of Galilee (six hundred and eighty feet minus) to the Dead Sea (thirteen hundred feet minus) is a distance of about sixty-five miles; therefore the descent is nearly ten feet to the mile, hence its name Jordan, the Downcomer. The difficulty of fording it, or of swimming across it on account of the whirling currents, added to the other physical features mentioned, simply emphasizes the idea of separation; it surely was a dividing line.

From the time when the Israelites crossed the river and entered the promised land down to the moment when Elijah smote the waters and crossed over, the river was a boundary. When Elisha smote the waters with the mantle of Elijah and returned to the land, the sons of the prophets said: "The spirit of Elijah doth rest on Elisha! And they came to meet him, and bowed themselves to the ground before him." This was the beginning of a new dispensation, the beginning of prophecy. The instrument of the Most High was to be not the state, not the laws, not even the church, but the spirit of one man.

Elisha was the first to use the river for a sacramental purpose; he said to Naaman the leper, "Go wash in Jordan seven times . . . and thou shalt be clean." Was not Israel's greatest river consecrated by these two acts most symbolic of religion—the washing by water and the gift of the Spirit?

Is it not more than passing strange that John, in this very place, called upon Israel to wash and be clean; and that where Elijah bequeathed his spirit to Elisha before he departed, John met his successor of whom he said, "There cometh He that is mightier than I after me, the latchet of whose shoes I am not worthy to stoop down and unloose. I indeed have baptized you with water, but He shall baptize you with the Holy Ghost"?

And so what was never a great Jewish river has become a very great Christian one.

From the Jordan ford we turned north-west toward Jericho. It was very hot and so we were compelled to ride slowly, when suddenly our horses pricked up their ears, began to neigh, and increased their speed until we came to a little stream of living water where the horses plunged in and drank. Upon discovering that the water was fit to drink, I fell prone on my face and drank till I could drink no more. For nearly a week I had tasted nothing but stale water purchased in Joppa. At last I understood what the Psalmist meant when he said, "As the hart panteth after the water brooks, so panteth my soul after thee, O God."

We pitched our tents near the source of this little brook, at the foot of the Judean hills, where the natives have constructed a small pool called the Sultan's Spring. Christians call it Elisha's Spring, because it is believed to be the spring into which he cast the salt and said, "Thus saith the Lord, I have healed these waters; there shall not be from thence any more death or barren land."

Near by are remains of a Roman road and a scanty ruin said to be the house of Rahab who saved the two men sent by Joshua to spy secretly. (Josh. ii.) West of the camp was a very high mountain which some say is the Mount of Temptation.

Early in the morning we turned our faces toward Jerusalem and began to ascend by the famous Jericho road. I have no doubt that our Lord and his disciples made use of this highway when "He steadfastly set his face to go to Jerusalem." (Luke ix, 51.)

On the way we passed by the ruins of an inn said to be the scene of the parable of the good Samaritan who helped the man who fell among thieves. I have no doubt of the truth of the latter assertion, for the thieves' descendants are there to-day. While the rest of the party went on, I climbed up one of the hills by the side of the road so that I could look down into the valley of the brook Cherith (I Kings xvii) where Elijah hid himself from Jezebel.

About half-way to Jerusalem we passed a poor little spring, the only one on the way, called the Apostle's Spring, near which were several hundreds of Russian pilgrims on their way to be baptized in the Jordan. They had stopped for rest and their mid-day meal, after which they arose and sang a thrilling chant of thanksgiving. Never have I been so moved by any choir or chorus in my own land. Their luncheon consisted of a crust of bread and a little tea. Weary and footsore, they slowly went on their way steadfastly toward the Jordan. Many were nearing the horizon of life, having toiled for many years to save enough to make this pilgrimage. In spite of everything there was a look upon their faces that I shall never forget. I felt almost ashamed to be on horseback.

This highway through the wilderness is very dreary, and the reflection of the sun's rays from the white limestone formation is almost unbearable. There is no shelter from the heat of the day, no tree, and only here and there a tuft of grass upon which the goats and sheep exist.

Oh! for the shade of a tree only for a little while! As this thought or prayer possessed me I turned, and before my eyes was a beautiful illustration of "The shadow of a great rock in a weary land." There before me were little kids and lambs resting in the shadow of a great rock. So comfortable were they, nestled together in that refreshing shadow, I had not the heart to drive them away, for I was thinking of the prophet Isaiah's words, "For thou hast been a strength to the poor, a strength to the needy in his distress, a refuge from the storm, a shadow from the heat." Surely, his mercy endureth forever.

As I stood near this great rock and gazed over Judea toward the Jordan I asked myself if the land was always as it is to-day—a land of stone, almost waterless, most of it treeless, here and there small patches where the vine might grow, no fields, except around Bethlehem, where grain would thrive, no farming as we understand it, nothing but here and there wandering shepherds searching for green pastures for their flocks?

Jeremiah answered my question when he said (xxxiii, 10, 12, 13), "Thus saith the Lord of Hosts; again in this place which is desolate without man and without beast, and in all the cities thereof, shall be an habitation of shepherds causing their flocks to lie down."

"In the cities of the mountains, in the cities of the vale, and in the cities of the south, and in the land of Benjamin, and in the places about Jerusalem, and in the cities of Judah, shall the flocks pass again under the hands of him that telleth them, saith the Lord."

Judah was destined to be pastoral, in Judah the Good Shepherd was born, in Judah the Good Shepherd gave his life for the sheep. (John x, 11, 15.)

"All we like sheep have gone astray; we have turned every

one to his own way; and the Lord hath laid on him the iniquity of us all." (Isa. liii, 6.)

"I have blotted out as a thick cloud, thy transgressions, and as a cloud, thy sins: return to me; for I have redeemed thee." (Isa. xliv, 22.)

Hot and weary, we slowly followed the Jericho road until we reached the little town of Bethany where Jesus often lodged; where he was anointed by Mary with the precious ointment; where he raised Lazarus from the dead; and where the ascension took place. The supposed ruins of the house of Mary and her sister Martha are still shown, and directly behind is a little mosque with a small dome, built by the Mohammedans over the tomb of Lazarus, for they regard him as a saint. There is nothing to prove that these two sites are genuine, nor is anything certain known regarding the places here visited by Christ. The town is situated on a hill, somewhat like Bethlehem, and presents a pleasing contrast to the desolate environs on account of the olive and fig trees which seem to thrive here as they used to in the time of Christ. (Matt. xxi, 19.)

As we left Bethany I saw two women at a mill grinding together just as Christ had said, "Two women shall be grinding together; the one shall be taken, and the other left." (Luke xvii, 35.)

Between Bethany and Jerusalem rises the Mount of Olives to an altitude of over two thousand seven hundred feet. It is stony and barren like most of the hills around Jerusalem, but the slopes are partially cultivated and there are still a few olive trees growing upon it.

Ezekiel and Zechariah both mentioned the Mount of Olives, and Matthew, Mark, and Luke often refer to it as a place frequented by Christ.

Quite a number of buildings have been erected upon the mount by the various religious sects, each claiming to have the true location of places associated with Christ during his sojourn in and near Jerusalem. So bitterly do the followers of the different Christian churches dispute about these and other things that they often come to blows.

While I was in the Holy Land, the priests of one church got into an altercation with those of another and fought each other with the brass-bound books of the church. Two were killed and many were seriously injured in a building consecrated to the worship of him who said, "By this shall all men know that ye are my disciples, if ye have love one to another."

The ignominy of this disgraceful incident was increased by the fact that Mohammedan soldiers were summoned to quell the disturbance. Now I know at least one reason why Mohammedans despise Christians. "Thou makest us a reproach to our neighbors, a scorn and a derision to them that are round about us." (Psalms xliv, 13.)

Had it not been for one of my favorite verses in the Bible, I should have then and there given up my camera crusade and my search for the truth in the Holy Land. "Let not your heart be troubled: ye believe in God, believe also in me."

The shock was so great, however, that I did not then go into Jerusalem; I looked over the city from the Mount of Olives, north-west toward Mizpah in the distance, and started north toward Samaria.

THE NORTH

AFTER a ride of about four hours we arrived at Bethel, one of the ancient sanctuaries of Israel and the lower boundary of Samaria. Here it was that Jacob had his wonderful vision, "and he called the name of that place Bethel: but the name of that city was called Luz at first."

Bethel means God's house. Of the ancient city nothing is left; the site of it is now occupied by a few stone hovels that shelter a disreputable gang of thieves. (Jer. vii, 11.) This is very much like the temple at Jerusalem in the time of Christ: "My house shall be called the house of prayer; but ye have made it a den of thieves." (Matt. xxi, 13.)

The great highway leading northward from Jerusalem to Samaria is the worst specimen of a road I have ever seen. Now I know why there were no chariots in Judea with the exception of those on two funereal occasions: first, when his servants carried Ahaziah in a chariot to Jerusalem from the plain of Megiddo; and, secondly, when Josiah was carried back to the same city. (II Kings ix, 28; II Chron. xxxv, 24.)

When people came down from Galilee or Samaria, they generally went down the Jordan valley and then took the Jericho road up to Jerusalem.

Not far north of Bethel there is a splendid view of the stony hills and fertile valleys of Samaria. Upon some of the high places or hills were little villages, almost indistinguishable, because the small houses were built of the same kind of stone so plentiful everywhere.

One never sees farm-houses scattered over the country as in other lands; they are always grouped close together on a high place as in ancient times. For as of old, even to this day, bands of Arab marauders swoop down upon these valleys, like a hawk upon its prey without warning, and they leave nothing of any value after them.

Upon one of the hills to the right were some large hewn stones; these indicated the site of Shiloh, the home of Eli and of the boy Samuel, the place where the whole congregation of the children of Israel assembled together and set up the tabernacle of the congregation.

The story of the capture of the Ark of the Covenant by the Philistines and its subsequent return to Shiloh is one of the most dramatic descriptions in the Bible. (I Sam. iv, v, vi, vii.)

It is not known when the destruction of Shiloh took place, although it is referred to in Jer. vii, 12, 14, and xxvi, 6.

Late in the afternoon, after riding all day through narrow, winding valleys, we entered a beautiful broad valley which is guarded by the great Mount Gerizim and Mount Ebal. The view was more impressive than any we had yet seen, quite in keeping with the entrance of the Israelites into the promised land and the great events which took place on and near these two mountains.

Sichem, or Shechem, the first capital of the land, and now the capital of the province, is situated in the pass between Mount Ebal and Mount Gerizim. Abraham and Jacob came at once to Sichem on their entrance into the promised land. Mount Ebal and Mount Gerizim together were the scene of the great inaugural service by all Israel on taking possession of the country.

The episode of Abimelech occurred at Shechem, and here was held the national assembly which resulted in the separation of the northern tribes from the southern. Jeroboam made Shechem his residence, while Rehoboam "made speed to get him up to his chariot, to flee to Jerusalem." To make the separation more complete and to prevent his people from going to Jerusalem to worship, Jeroboam set up a golden image in Dan and another in Bethel.

The environs of Shechem are very fertile and there are copious springs, but the water is not pleasant to drink because it contains so much carbonate of lime in solution. Many of these springs become exhausted during the summer months.

A few of the descendants of the ancient Samaritans still dwell here, and in their synagogue they jealously guard a very old codex of the Pentateuch. Although all these things are intensely interesting, they are eclipsed by a "parcel of ground that Jacob gave to his son Joseph. Now Jacob's well was there." (John iv, 5, 6; Gen. xxxiii, 19.)

From the eastern slope of Mount Ebal there is a magnificent view of Mount Gerizim and the valley to the south. Immediately below Mount Ebal lies the little village of Ain Askar, or Sychar, while a little farther on is "a parcel of ground" surrounded by a stone wall, built by the Greeks who now own this property. Within the enclosure is the ruin of a very old church, built many centuries ago, directly over Jacob's well.

There is not the shadow of a doubt about this being the well. Jews, Christians, and Muslims all agree that it is the well of Jacob.

In order to reach this sacred spot, it is necessary to climb down some steep steps into a small chapel which was built directly over the well itself. As I entered I felt, as I did in no other place in the Holy Land, that I was in a holy place; for this was the well upon which Jesus sat, being wearied with his journey, and there came a woman of Samaria to draw water. "Jesus saith unto her, Give me to drink." After a wonderful conversation, full of spiritual meaning, the woman said, "I know that Messias cometh, which is called Christ: when he is come, he will tell us all things."

"Jesus saith unto her, I that speak unto thee am He." (John iv, 3–26.)

Long ago when Moses turned aside to see why the bush was not burnt, God called to him and said, "Draw not nigh hither; put off thy shoes from off thy feet, for the place whereon thou standest is holy ground."

"Moreover he said, I am the God of thy father, the God of Abraham, the God of Isaac, and the God of Jacob. And Moses hid his face; for he was afraid to look upon God." (Ex. iii, 3–6.)

"And God said unto Moses, I AM THAT I AM." (Ex. iii, 14.)

"Jesus said unto them, Verily, verily, I say unto you, Before Abraham was, I am." (John viii, 58.) "I am Alpha and Omega. The beginning and the end, saith the Lord which is, and which was, and which is to come, the Almighty." (Rev. i, 8.)

Overwhelmed with emotions that surpass description, I slowly left the well of Jacob. "Whosoever drinketh of the water that I shall give him shall never thirst; but the water that I shall give him shall be in him a well of water springing up into everlasting life." (John iv, 14.)

"And whosoever will, let him take the water of life freely." (Rev. xxii, 17.)

That curbstone over Jacob's well was my "Ebenezer"; for there the Lord helped me. There, at that stone, came to me the "Peace of God which passeth all understanding."

As the shepherd puts a stone in his sling and casts it at a wandering sheep, as I have already mentioned, so it seems to me God Almighty often throws a stone that it may cause the wanderer to look up. "For whom the Lord loveth he chasteneth." (Heb. xii, 6.)

"Blessed is the man whom thou chasteneth, O Lord, and teachest him out of thy law." (Psalm xciv, 12.)

Only a short distance from the well is the village of Sychar, where a Samaritan woman lived who went to the well to draw water. I walked through the village and chanced to see a Samaritan woman with a water jar on her head about to go to draw water.

My camera caught a picture that will live with me forever, a woman of Samaria, carrying her little child in her bosom, standing in a doorway which had been sprinkled with the blood of a lamb—for it was at the time of the feast of the Passover—"There cometh a woman of Samaria to draw water." It was early in the morning that she came out of the door to go and draw water, quite in keeping with the old law of Moses: "Draw out and take you a lamb according to your families, and kill the passover."

"And ye shall take a bunch of hyssop, and dip it in the blood that is in the bason, and strike the lintel and the two side-posts with the blood that is in the bason; and none of you shall go out at the door of his house until the morning." (Ex. xii, 21, 22.)

So even to this day do they keep this, the law of the old covenant.

"Behold, the days come, saith the Lord, that I will make a new covenant with the house of Israel and with the house of Judah: not according to the covenant that I made with their fathers in the day that I took them by the hand to bring them out of the land of Egypt." (Jer. xxxi, 31, 32.)

"And as they were eating, Jesus took bread, and blessed it, and brake it, and gave it to the disciples and said, Take, eat; this is my body."

"And he took the cup and gave thanks, and gave it to them, saying, Drink ye all of it; For this is my blood of the new testament, which is shed for many for the remission of sins." (Matt. xxvi, 26, 27, 28.)

"Behold the Lamb of God, which taketh away the sin of the world." (John i, 29.)

"Blessing, and honour, and glory, and power, be unto him that sitteth upon the throne, and unto the Lamb for ever and ever." (Rev. v, 13.)

After reading the fifty-third chapter of Isaiah, I turned my face northward toward Sebaste, the city of Samaria, built upon a hill like most of the fortresses of Samaria. As we approached the hill upon which the modern town of Sebaste is situated, wide and fertile valleys stretched out in every direction before us. This is the striking feature of Samaria, its openness.

The landscape was refreshing after the desolate hills and dales of Judea.

The history of this northern part of Israel is extremely interesting, although it can hardly be looked upon as the Holy Land in the same sense as Judea or Galilee. The patriarchs came here first, and then made their homes in Hebron; the earliest sanctuaries of Israel were here, but Jerusalem became the centre of church and state. At first the prophets and heroes of the north shone resplendent, but those of Judah endured and the kingship remained with Judah.

There is nothing in all Samaria that appeals to the pilgrim of to-day like the place where Jesus rested as he went through it, and he passed through it only of necessity. (John iv, 4.)

Omri bought the hill Samaria of Shemer for two talents of silver, about $3,285, equal to ten times that amount to-day in purchasing power.

And he called the name of the city which he built after the name of Shemer, the owner of the hill, Shomeron, which is the Hebrew for Samaria.

The first capital of Israel was Tirzah, a little to the northeast of Shechem. Samaria was the second capital and the scene of many events under the kings. It was captured by the Syrians, also by the Assyrians, and rebuilt by Herod the Great, who named the city Sebaste (Augusta) in honor of

Augustus. The only remains which pertain to his time are a row of columns which probably stood near the temple, erected in honor of the Emperor.

According to tradition, John the Baptist was beheaded here, but Josephus says that this occurred at Machærus (Mukaur), a fortified town east of the Dead Sea, where the unhappy survivors of the destruction of Jerusalem fled for refuge.

North of Sebaste the valleys widen and finally become great plains such as Megiddo (Esdraelon) and Jezreel, which extend from the sea on the west to the Jordan. This is the reason why few invaders were successfully resisted.

The most interesting effect of this openness of Samaria is the use of the chariot, as related in the Old Testament. Ahab rode in his chariot from Carmel to Jezreel (I Kings xvii, 44); his chariot was his funeral car from Ramoth-Gilead to Samaria (I Kings xxii, 29). Jehu rode in a chariot to Jezreel, and the watchman said to Joram, "The driving is like the driving of Jehu, the son of Nimshi; for he driveth furiously" (II Kings ix, 16); Jehu pursued Ahaziah, the son of Ahab, and after Ahaziah's death, his servants carried his body in a chariot to Jerusalem (II Kings ix, 27, 28); Jehu rode from Jezreel to Samaria (Sebaste) and took up Jehonadab into his chariot and boastfully said, "Come with me and see my zeal for the Lord"; and then Naaman made the long drive from Damascus to the house of Elisha in Samaria, and then rode all the way back again (II Kings v); the King of Syria sent a great host with horses and chariots to surround Dothan in order to capture Elisha. (II Kings vi, 13 *ff*.)

If one reads these accounts carefully, the cause of the fall and destruction of open Samaria can readily be discerned.

About two hours north of Sebaste we passed the site of Dothan where Joseph's brethren conspired against him to slay him (Gen. xxxvii, 15), and we camped near the town of Jenin (Engannin), situated on the edge of the plain of Jezreel, the Greek name of which is Esdraelon, while in the Old Testament it is Megiddo. This plain was the battle-field of the great empires of the world at one time or another, but always the prey and pasture of the wild bands of Arabs who came every spring as regularly as the seasons, and a few years ago the peasants got rid of these Arab marauders, only to be bought up by rich Greeks from Beyrout.

Thus we see the "mutability, the irrevocable lot, of man and all his works." (Irving.)

As we entered the plain of Jezreel we met a caravan laden with goods from the Far East. This made us realize that we were approaching the place where the great highways connecting the east and the west, the south and the north crossed each other.

Upon the highest point of the plain stands the miserable village of Zerin, the ancient Jezreel, a town of Issachar, the son of Jacob and Leah. When Jacob called his sons together to tell them what was to befall them, he said of this one: "Issachar is a strong ass couching down between two burdens: and he saw that rest was good, and the land that it was pleasant; and bowed his shoulder to bear, and became a servant unto tribute." (Gen. xlix, 14, 15.)

This is one of the many passages in the Bible so hard to understand because we have not the customs nor the environment necessary to understand fully the figurative language used in the East even to this day. It means that this plain is stretched out between the hills just as an ass stretches himself out whenever he gets the opportunity to take a rest; and, moreover, it is very fertile and therefore pleasant to one accustomed to the stony hills or sheepfolds; but it must be paid for by hard work and by paying tribute as a vassal. That has been the history of this plain.

Jezreel was the home of the infamous Jezebel, from whom Elijah fled in terror.

The other references given in connection with the chariots will quite suffice the reader.

Near Jezreel we saw some Arabs ploughing the rich soil with ploughs made after the ancient pattern, simply the curved stump of a small tree shod with a point of iron. Behind the plough walks the ploughman, carrying in one hand a long stick with a sharp point for the purpose of pricking the oxen to make them work, just as we use a whip upon a lazy animal to-day. It would certainly be hard for them to "kick against the pricks." This is used figuratively in Acts ix, 5; v, 39, and vii, 51.

The plain of Jezreel descends gradually to the Jordan where there are several fords, one of which Naaman must have used when he came from Damascus to seek the prophet Elisha in the hope of being cured of his leprosy. Perhaps the very one used as an illustration is where he washed in the Jordan seven times and was healed.

Toward the east the plain gradually rises until it culminates in the lofty ridge of Mount Carmel close by the sea. In the north rises Mount Tabor like a great round dome. These two mountains are frequently used in the Scriptures as symbols of strength or certainty. From the earliest times Mount Carmel was used as a sanctuary; there was an altar to Baal, and likewise one to Jehovah, which was broken down. The contest which took place here between the prophets of Baal and the prophet of the Lord is recorded in the most dramatic manner in I Kings xviii.

North of the great plain lies the province of Galilee about which hover so many holy memories.

As we approached Nazareth we crossed the great caravan route from Egypt to Damascus and found ourselves at the very cross-roads of this part of the world. Nazareth is situated in a kind of basin surrounded on the north by hills. From the town itself there is no view at all, but from the tops of the hills the views in every direction are wonderful. To the south Esdraelon lies before you so rich in important events, and then Mount Carmel and the place of Elisha's sacrifice; to the east the valley of the Jordan and the range of Gilead; to the west the Great Sea with the ships of Tarshish; to the north a landscape of hills and dales more fertile and better watered than any other section of Palestine; to this add the great routes which pass through or near by Nazareth and you will no longer wonder why the boy Jesus was brought up here. The view from the hills is like a map of Old Testament history, while over these roads passed all the nations of the earth, bringing news and gossip from everywhere just as to-day.

So Nazareth was not an obscure, secluded village; it was the very opposite, and he grew up under these conditions, "in all points tempted like as we are, yet without sin." I am convinced that he was in this land but not of it.

In the town there is but one spring or fountain, as it is called in that land, where I have no doubt Mary the mother of Jesus used to go to draw water just as the women of Nazareth do to this day. The natives call it the Well of Mary. The tiled roofs of the modern town show the Frankish or European invasion of Nazareth.

The first town we saw after leaving Nazareth was Cana of Galilee, where the first miracle that is recorded was performed, the changing of the water into wine at a wedding feast.

After a pleasant ride over a road that wound its way around and over many hills, we came to the "high mountain" named the Mount of the Beatitudes, where probably the Sermon on the Mount was preached to the multitude. Standing on this mount, my voice was easily heard by my friends scattered about the fields below. While the acoustics of this place would permit many to hear his wonderful sermon, only those heard who had ears to hear.

To the east, far below this mount, lay the glittering blue Lake of Galilee in the deep valley of the Jordan, at this point six hundred and eighty feet below the level of the sea. As I rode over the same road that Christ used so long ago, it seemed to me that again was I in a holy place, for nearly all of the ministry of Christ was accomplished in this vicinity.

The contrasts presented by the situation of the Lake of Galilee and its surroundings are startling. Here in this deep

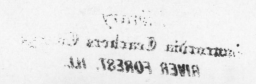

valley or trench lies the lake of clear fresh water, full of fish, the color of the water a sparkling blue, the surface of which is often broken into little ripples by the cool breezes from the snow-capped Lebanon and Hermon, and sometimes lashed into furious waves by the sudden gusts of wind that swoop down upon the lake from the sterile volcanic heights which almost encompass the whole shore.

How different it must have been when Christ went about these shores and hills doing good. Then the hills were covered with trees and the shores were lined with villages and large, busy towns, for people were attracted to this beautiful lake from every land and nation.

Trees and plants of the temperate and the tropical zones could here grow in close proximity because of the steep slope of the hills which fall from an altitude of four thousand feet above the sea to six hundred and eighty feet below at the shores of the Lake of Galilee.

Josephus, who described this province which he governed only a few years after the time of Christ, writes: "The plain of Gennesaret had soil so fruitful that all sorts of trees would grow upon it, for the temper of the air is so well blended that it suits those many sorts, especially walnuts which require the colder air (relatively to the rest), and flourish there in great plenty. There are palm trees also which grow best in hot air; fig trees also, and olives grow near them, which require an air more temperate."

The few little gardens I saw in my wanderings around the lake gave proof of this luxuriance which is accentuated by wealth of wild flowers everywhere, except in the vicinity of the hot springs near the town of Tiberias. This town, built on the site of an ancient city by Herod and named after the Roman Emperor, is the only one remaining of the many cities of other days. It is of little interest to the Christian and was detested by the Jew, because they considered the place defiled. Perhaps it is for this reason, and because it was new, that it is not mentioned in the ministry of Christ. At all events, this section of the shore of the lake is unhealthy and not as pleasant as the parts farther north.

The hot springs or baths of Tiberias lie close to the shore about a mile below Tiberias. In spite of the changes everywhere which have obliterated names and sites, these springs have preserved their reputation and name. Joshua called them Hammath and to-day the natives speak of them as Hammam Tabariyeh, and, as of old, many are brought here to be cured of their ills. The springs are built over with bathhouses which are not at all inviting and indescribably dirty, like most of the native structures in this vicinity.

One day I chanced to see four fishing-boats on the lake, an unusual sight to-day, and I thought of other days when there must have been many who made fishing their business. Near Capernaum I watched the fishermen casting their nets and I drew near in time to see them haul the net, but that time "they caught nothing." How close that brought me to the time when Jesus stood on that shore and said, "Children, have ye any meat? They answered him, No. And he said unto them, Cast the net on the right side of the ship, and ye shall find. They cast therefore, and now they were not able to draw it for the multitude of fishes." (John xxi.)

The exact site of Capernaum is still in dispute, so we cannot say just where the home of Christ was, but it was somewhere in this immediate vicinity where I stood and watched the fishermen.

How singular it was that Christ sought for his disciples among the free hardy fishermen, independent, yet not wealthy, simple and receptive. And Jesus said unto them, "Come ye after me, and I will make you to become fishers of men."

We entered a boat and sailed to the place where the Jordan flows into the Sea of Galilee. Beyond the eastern bank of the river lay a plain covered with grass and low bushes. This probably is where Christ fed the multitude with the loaves and fishes.

Bethsaida probably stood just a short distance up the river, but there is not a vestige of it left now. And so it is with Chorazin and Capernaum, a complete fulfilment of the upbraiding of "the cities wherein most of his mighty works were done, because they repented not." (Matt. xi, 20–24.)

"And thou Capernaum, which art exalted unto heaven, shalt be brought down to hell: for if the mighty works, which have been done in thee, had been done in Sodom, it would have remained until this day."

Our little company were loath to turn from these places of sacred memory to continue the journey along the route to Damascus.

The valley of the upper Jordan offers little of interest in the way of towns or life, and yet there I saw the "still waters" and "green pastures." The children of the East come up here with their cattle and their tents in search of pasture just as they have done since the time or before the time of Moses. Their black tents made of camel's hair by the women are so constructed that they may be quickly set up and as speedily struck, as it were in a moment. How great must have been the terror of Ben-hadad, King of Syria, and his hosts when "they arose and fled in the twilight, and left their tents and their horses, and their asses, even the camp as it was, and fled for their life." (II Kings vii, 7.)

These nomads are troublesome people to deal with, for they have inherited the tendency to relieve passers-by of their worldly goods and possessions. It is therefore well to travel with a party and not alone.

After paying tribute to the sheik, according to ancient custom, we continued up by the waters of Merom with the great Mount Hermon in the background dominating the marshy valley of the Jordan, now only seven feet below sea-level. There were many little brooks flowing down from the spurs of Lebanon, which still was hidden from us. It was interesting to watch the goatherds and the shepherds lead their flocks down to the still waters, and they separated the sheep from the goats.

Above the waters of Merom the valley suddenly narrows and the Jordan flows for some distance through a wild, rocky ravine which is spanned by a dilapidated stone bridge built by the Romans. As far as the eye could see, the river banks were resplendent with oleanders in full bloom.

After crossing the bridge we began the ascent of the foothills of Mount Hermon. We passed a magnificent oak tree under which were several tombs. The oak tree is frequently mentioned in the Scriptures; Deborah was buried under an oak; Joshua set up a great stone under an oak; Jacob hid all the strange gods and the ear-rings under an oak; Absalom's hair caught hold of the oak; it seemed to be regarded with great reverence in the olden days by every one, even as by the Muslims to-day.

After a steady ascent for more than an hour we arrived at Tell-el-kadi, one of the supposed sites of Laish, which the Danites took for their city.

About an hour farther on is Banias which I think is more likely to be the site of ancient Dan, for Banias seems to be the key to this whole district. Trees and undergrowth were most luxuriant and hid from view the gushing, headlong stream which we soon crossed by means of an old Roman bridge. A few steps beyond the bridge a great cliff one hundred and fifty feet high suddenly confronts you. In the cliff is a great cavern from which the Jordan issues, full born, with the sound of joyous, bubbling water. The mouth of the cavern is now almost concealed by masses of broken rocks that have broken away from the cliff for many centuries.

No one takes care of this wonderful spot now, but the many niches cut deep into the walls of the cliff indicate that this was a sanctuary in by-gone days, where man fell on his face and worshipped his God. It might have been Baal or Pan, the gods of the Greeks or of the Romans, of the Syrians and of the Assyrians; no matter by what name, the individual here gave thanks for the blessed gift of pure water, clear as crystal. Here, from the very foundations of snowy Mount Hermon, springs forth that river, the like of which there is not another on this earth.

In its geographical aspect the Jordan is most remarkable, for it rises at an altitude of over one thousand one hundred and fifty feet, flows through an extraordinary trench or valley most of the way below sea-level until it empties into the Dead Sea one thousand three hundred feet below the level of the ocean.

In its religious aspect it stands alone, for it is the symbol of the beginning of the Christian life, baptism, and the ending, the waters of death, which separate him from the promised land. Although the river is referred to directly only a few times in the Bible, the symbolical references are almost without number.

This visit to the source of the Jordan was a revelation to me, for here, surrounded by the images of various gods, stood Jesus Christ himself and his disciples (for they had sought refuge from the hostility of the Jews in this place Banias, which was Cæsarea Philippi), and he asked his disciples, saying, "Whom do men say that I the son of man am? And they said, Some say that thou art John the Baptist: some, Elias; and others, Jeremias, or one of the prophets. He saith unto them, But whom say ye that I am? And Simon Peter answered and said, Thou art the Christ, the son of the living God." (Matt. xvi, 13, 16.)

Is it not wonderful that this declaration should have been made in the presence, as it were, of the gods of other religions? And especially near that temple where the Emperor Augustus was worshipped as God?

It was here that he resolved to return to Jerusalem "and suffer many things," so "He steadfastly set his face to go to Jerusalem."

As I stood here at the source of the Jordan looking at this pure stream welling forth to bless the earth, and remembered that on this very spot was made the first confession of man that Christ was the Son of God, one verse of Revelation came to me and has lived with me, "And he shewed me a pure river of water of life, clear as crystal, proceeding out of the throne of God and of the lamb."

In all probability Christ never went farther north than Banias or Cæsarea Philippi. Although Damascus is not in the Holy Land, it is so closely connected with its history that even if Paul had not gone there and boldly preached Christ after his conversion it is worth the time and trouble, being only sixteen hours from Banias.

(Since the completion of the railways, Damascus is easily reached either from Haifa or Beyrout.)

As I journeyed over the ancient road, I read the account of Paul's journey to Damascus. (Acts ix.) How vivid it all was as I entered the city and walked through the street that is called straight and then saw the Christian section, which has never recovered from the terrible devastation to which it was subjected in 1860, when more than six thousand Christians were massacred!

After visiting the most attractive bazaars, the finest in the Far East, I passed through an old-fashioned gate and walked along the road outside the walls of the city and was shown the window through which Paul was let down by the wall in a basket. Now as this wall was built by the Turks centuries after Paul visited Damascus, this could not possibly be the window.

This is one of the many instances where this, that, or the other place is pointed out by the various churches in the Holy Land as the true site without a scintilla of proof and often in direct contradiction of well-known historical facts. I mention this as a warning to any intending to visit Palestine.

"And the king said unto him, How many times shall I adjure thee that thou tell me nothing but that which is true in the name of the Lord?" (I Kings xxii, 16.)

Damascus has always been regarded as an earthly paradise by the Arabs who describe paradise as being a garden full of fruit trees, watered by a stream of flowing water, yielding all manner of delicious fruits ever ripe for the delectation of the faithful. We, who are blessed with green hills and dales, with gurgling brooks everywhere so numerous that their music becomes common and is hardly noticed, cannot appreciate the emotions of those who live in, and wander over, the hot sands of the desert when they suddenly come upon Damascus with its gardens and orchards watered by the rivers Barada (Abana) and Nahr el Awaj (Pharpar).

From the top of a house I looked over the city, with its many minarets, and the river Barada toward Mount Hermon, and could distinctly see the triple peaks covered with snow. Many of the best authorities agree that the transfiguration of Christ took place upon this "high mountain apart."

This seems very probable to me, for Christ stayed several days at Banias, that place of refuge, just at the base of Mount

Hermon, and the ascent of the mountain is not difficult. (Compare Matt. xvii, 1; Mark ix, 2; Luke ix, 28.)

From the top of the mountain one can see nearly all of Syria. The haze which seems to be ever present in the low valley of the Jordan prevents a distinct view farther than the Sea or Lake of Galilee. Tabor and Carmel were hardly distinguishable. The mountains of Lebanon seemed to stretch out in every direction like the roots of a great oak. Hosea must have seen this view, for he writes: "I will be as the dew unto Israel: he shall grow as the lily, and cast forth his roots as Lebanon." (Hosea xiv, 5.)

It is on account of these mountains that Galilee has more dew and rain than Samaria and Judea.

Having seen these great mountains of the north, I returned to the Mount of Olives so often visited by Christ and looked once more toward Jerusalem.

JERUSALEM

From the top of the Mount of Olives the city lies before you "builded as a city that is compact together" upon an island of rocks surrounded by deep valleys, except on the north. The temple and the palaces of the kings have disappeared; its mighty towers have been laid low; there is nothing left to indicate the former greatness of Judah's capital except her situation.

The city could easily be attacked and taken, but it could not be held unless all the neighboring hills had been captured beforehand; therefore I think that is what the psalmist had in mind in the beginning of his beautiful song: "I will lift mine eyes unto the hills, from whence cometh my help." (Psalm cxxi.)

Psalm xlviii: "Great is the Lord, and greatly to be praised in the city of our God, in the mountain of his holiness. Beautiful for situation, the joy of the whole earth, is Mount Zion, on the sides of the north, the city of the great king."

Truly the situation of Mount Zion, where the temple stood, is beautiful, but now desolate. The sad prediction of Christ is fulfilled: "O Jerusalem, Jerusalem, which killest the prophets, and stonest them that are sent unto thee; how often would I have gathered thy children together, as a hen doth gather her brood under her wings, and ye would not! Behold, your house is left unto you desolate: and verily I say unto you, Ye shall not see me, until the time come when ye shall say, Blessed is he that cometh in the name of the Lord." (Luke xiii, 34, 35; compare Isa. xxx, 15.)

One Friday I stood in the wailing-place of the Jews and heard their sad litany:

"For the palace that lies desolate: *We sit in solitude and mourn.*

For the walls that are overthrown: *We sit in solitude and mourn.*

For our majesty that is departed: *We sit in solitude and mourn.*

We pray thee, have mercy on Zion!—*Gather the children of Jerusalem.*"

Profoundly moved, I turned away, filled with compassion and wonder. They were using the very words uttered by Christ! And they will continue doing so "until the time come." The miracle of to-day! The Jew! (Deut. iv, 25–40.)

How do those who decry miracles explain the Jew, scattered to the uttermost parts of the earth? Dwelling among all peoples, yet distinct and separate.

"Behold, the Lord's hand is not shortened, that it cannot save; neither is his ear heavy, that it cannot hear: But your iniquities have separated between you and your God, and your sins have hid his face from you, that he will not hear." (Isa. lix, 1, 2.) But the time will come as predicted, for "he will not always chide: neither will he keep his anger forever." (Ps. ciii)

"I will rejoice in Jerusalem, and the joy of my people: and the voice of weeping shall be no more heard in her, nor the voice of crying." (Isa. lxv, 19.)

The great wall of the wailing-place, against which the Jews lean in their sorrow, is exposed for a distance of about one hundred and fifty feet and is fifty-six feet high above the present level of the pavement. Some of the stones are huge and show the eroding effect of time.

From the wailing-place I went to the site of the temple, near the place where David built an altar unto the Lord. This large quadrangular place, now called the Haram esh-Sherif, is paved with great blocks of stone. Scattered over this great stone platform are many places of prayer for the faithful Muslims, for they are now in possession of this, one of the most interesting spots in the world. All creeds agree that the sanctuary of the Lord God Almighty stood here until the fulfilment of the prophecy in I Kings ix, 7.

"Then will I cut off Israel out of the land which I have given them; and this house, which I have hallowed for my name, will I cast out of my sight; and Israel shall be a proverb and a byword among all people."

"And Jesus said unto them, See ye not all these things? Verily I say unto you, There shall not be left here one stone upon another, that shall not be thrown down." (Matt. xxiv, 2.)

Near the centre of this platform is a Mohammedan mosque, called the Mosque of Omar, which stands directly over the dome of the rock. The Mohammedans will not allow excavations or investigations to be made here, which is a great pity, for I believe that upon this sacred rock once stood the Ark of the Covenant and that the great altar of sacrifice was here.

According to Jewish tradition, Abraham and Melchizedek sacrificed here; Abraham was about to sacrifice his only son Isaac upon this place, which he called Jehovah-jireh, "the Lord will provide"; and on this rock was written the great and unspeakable name of God, which, according to tradition, Jesus succeeded in reading and so was able to work his miracles. These are a few of the traditions which have been handed down from generation to generation, and the Jews of to-day cling to them most tenaciously.

Solomon's temple must have been magnificent according to the description given in II Chronicles; the second temple, erected after the return from exile, was inferior; while the third temple, which Herod built, was superior to that of Solomon. Many have endeavored to reconstruct and reproduce the temple in word pictures or drawings from the very unsatisfactory description given by Josephus.

The present structure is a fine example of Arabian architecture following Byzantine designs. This beautiful building produced such an impression on the templars in the Middle Ages that they thought it was the temple of Solomon and carried the design back to Europe with them. Young Raphael saw this design and used it in his famous painting of the Sposalizio, the nuptials of the Virgin, now in the Brera Gallery at Milan.

I believe, however, that it was the purpose of God Almighty to destroy the temple so utterly that man would turn from the contemplation of sticks and stones unto him who said, "Destroy this temple, and in three days I will raise it up." (John ii, 19.)

St. Stephen said just before he was stoned to death: "But Solomon built him an house. Howbeit the most High dwelleth not in temples made with hands." (Acts vii, 47.)

From the great stone square where once stood the temple of other days, I walked to the Church of the Holy Sepulchre. The present building was erected in 1810 over the remains of several other buildings, the earliest of which was consecrated in the year 336 A. D.

The traditions, legends, and stories which have been woven about this shrine would fill many volumes, and the task of repeating them is quite beyond the scope of my camera crusade. The photographic plates in my camera refused to record the impressions of the dark, gloomy chapels and other things in the various parts of the interior of the building— would that I could say that of my heart and mind.

The Greek, the Latin, the Armenian, and the Coptic churches, each own portions of the interior, and, sad to relate, a guard of Mohammedan soldiers is posted there to keep order among the Christians. During the Easter festivals— for there are two, one the Latin, the other the Greek—the Church of the Holy Sepulchre and the city are crowded with pilgrims of every nationality. After one experience in the church I preferred to stay outside.

In the little square south of the entrance I saw the Greek ceremony of the washing of feet. Every nook and crevice about the square was occupied by spectators,

One day as I was walking through the streets I saw a house with a "large upper room," and it made me think of

Christ's instructions to the two disciples, "Go ye into the city, and there shall meet you a man bearing a pitcher of water: follow him, . . . and he will show you a large upper room furnished and prepared: there make ready for us."

I went up into the room; it was the guest-chamber of the good man of the house, and I have no doubt that it was much like the one in which Christ and his disciples kept the Passover, and instituted the sacrament of the holy communion. "This do in remembrance of me." It seemed as though I was to have two things to remember, for under that room was a manger just like the one where Christ our passover was born.

Not far from this house I was shown a pool far below the present level of the street, near the sheep market. It is called the Pool of Bethesda. It appears to correspond with the description given in John v, 2, but there is nothing to prove that this is the pool where an angel went down at a certain season and troubled the water. And this difficulty meets one everywhere in Jerusalem, and it will not be removed until the whole city has been thoroughly excavated, a thing that is utterly impossible under the present government.

I made very few photographs within the city walls, and I received very few impressions pleasant to remember or that were edifying.

One night as I sat in my tent on the Mount of Olives reading descriptions of Jerusalem in the Old Testament, I read Psalms xlviii, 12, 13, 14. "Walk about Zion, and go round about her: tell the towers thereof. Mark ye well her bulwarks, consider her palaces; that ye may tell it to the generation following. For this God is our God for ever and ever: he will be our guide even unto death."

It seemed to be a command. Early in the morning I entered Jerusalem for the last time by the gate where St. Stephen was stoned to death, walked rapidly through the quaint arched streets until I reached the Joppa gate; there I began my walk round about Jerusalem.

"Tell the towers thereof." Alas, there is only one left, called the Tower of David. It stands high up above the well-preserved west wall of the city.

David said "For thou hast been a shelter for me, and a strong tower from the enemy." Just below David's tower is the Pool of Gihon, built by Hezekiah so as to preserve the water of the brook Gihon. Jerusalem is really destitute of water except one poor little spring. The inhabitants depend upon rain water caught in cisterns. I then walked south beyond the valley of Hinnom, and from a hill looked northeast over the valley toward the south-eastern slope of Mount Zion, the Tyropœan valley, with the village of Siloam on the right and the Mount of Olives with its Russian tower in the background.

Then I walked down into the Valley of Hinnom, which was the ancient southern border of the city of David. To the left of this valley rises the Mount of Evil Counsel, where the last view was obtained. It is so named because Caiaphas possessed a country house here in which he consulted with the Jews how he might kill Jesus.

It was in this valley that children were at one time sacrificed to Moloch; therefore the place was called Tophet, the place of fire. The Jews detested the place and called it Gehenna. To the left, under the Mount of Evil Counsel, are many tombs cut deep into the rock.

This valley runs nearly east and west. Turning to the north, the valley of the brook Kidron leads by the village of Siloam to the Pool of Siloam. I was a church organist for many years and often played that hymn, "By Cool Siloam's Shady Rill." I will never play that again. Whoever wrote that hymn had never smelt that pool. Perhaps it was not so bad in David's time.

Just above this is the Tyropœan Valley, now filled up with rubbish. This valley is not mentioned in the Bible; the name is Greek and means the valley of dung; it is most appropriately named. In David's time this valley was much deeper than it is now and was probably the western boundary of the city of David. From the Pool of Siloam the view south is very picturesque. On the right the Valley of Hinnom enters the King's Dale and meets the valley of the brook Kidron. At the junction of these two valleys is a well, covered with a domed structure, which the Muslims without reason call Job's Well. I am convinced that this is the well by En-rogel, where Jonathan and Ahimaaz went down into a well and a woman covered the well's mouth so that the thing was not known. (II Sam. xvii, 15–22.)

From the well which I prefer to call En-rogel the view up the Kidron Valley is striking. On the right is the village of Siloah, or Siloam, then the valley of the brook Kidron, with the corner of the temple wall high up on the left. It was across this valley that David and all his followers fled from his son Absalom.

A little farther up the valley is the only spring in or near Jerusalem; it is called the Spring of Mary. In the olden times it was called the Spring of Gihon. Here I saw little girls go down and fill water-bottles made of the whole skin of a goat, and with charming grace carry their heavy burden to the village of Siloam. Let me here warn every one to be careful and never drink any water in Jerusalem unless they see it boiled.

These skin bottles are used all over the land just as they were in the olden time, not only for water, but for wine also. An old skin would not stand the pressure of new wine; hence the saying, "Neither do men put new wine into old bottles."

Beyond the Spring of Mary, the Kidron Valley begins to open. High above on the left is the corner of the temple wall; directly in front, in the bottom of the valley, which is sometimes called the Valley of Jehoshaphat, there are many tombs, of which three have important names attached to them: the tomb of Absalom, of Jehoshaphat, and of Zacharias. I simply say that these names are attached to them.

Just beyond these tombs (and it may be well to call attention to the fact that all the tombs next to the city walls on the left are Mohammedan tombs, while those on the right side of the valley are Jewish) the Golden Gate comes into view. "Then he brought me back the way of the gate of the outward sanctuary which looketh toward the east; and it was shut.

Then said the Lord unto me: This gate shall be shut, it shall not be opened, and no man shall enter in by it; because the Lord the God of Israel hath entered in by it, therefore it shall be shut. It is for the prince; the prince, he shall sit in it to eat bread before the Lord; he shall enter by the way of the porch of that gate and shall go out by the way of the same." (Ezek. xliv, 1–3.)

This indicates that the Golden Gate was shut up at a very early period. During the time of the Crusades this gate was opened on Palm Sunday, and the great procession with palm branches entered the city by this gate from the Mount of Olives.

After capturing the city, the Mohammedans closed the gate again and it has not been opened since. They have a very curious tradition that they will hold Jerusalem until a Christian conqueror opens the gate, enters, and captures the city. They also say that the columns of the gate were presented to Solomon by the Queen of Sheba.

The reason the valley below the gate is so full of tombs and graves is that both the Jews and the Mohammedans believe that the resurrection will begin here. The Mohammedans have a remarkable idea of the last day. On that day a hair from the beard of the prophet will be stretched from the Golden Gate to the top of the Mount of Olives. Christ will sit at one end and Mohammed at the other as judges. Those who succeed in crossing on that slender bridge will reach eternal bliss, whereas those who have no faith will slip and fall down to perdition in the valley below, which will open to receive them into the bottomless pit. The faithful, however, will have no difficulty, for they will be sustained by the two angels appointed by Allah to guard them.

Almost directly across the valley from the Golden Gate is the Garden of Gethsemane, a quiet place with aged olive trees now surrounded by flower beds tenderly cared for by Franciscan monks. It is situated at the base of the Mount of Olives and is about a Sabbath day's journey from Jerusalem, so it was far enough away from the city to be a retreat from the crowds and excitement during the feast of the Passover.

"And when Jesus had spoken these words, he went forth with his disciples over the brook Cedron (Kidron), where was a garden, into which he entered, and his disciples." (John xviii, 1.)

Here he came, despised and rejected of men, a man of sorrows and acquainted with grief, to pray. And such a prayer! Think of the agony of the One without sin taking upon himself the sin of the world!

That night, in that garden, he was betrayed.

As I stood in that garden nearly two thousand years after that awful night and looked upon those old olive trees which may have witnessed that betrayal of the Son of man, I wondered, ay! I wondered, I shall always wonder!

From the Garden of Gethsemane I walked around the north-east corner of the wall of the city and along the north wall till I came to the Damascus Gate. There, seated about the gate, were all kinds of men, some gossiping or arguing, others trading and bargaining, and some just loafing.

The inevitable beggar was also there, even a poor leper. Through the gate came one of the sons of Levi dressed in the raiment peculiar to the time of the feast of the Passover and wearing a curious fur turban. It seemed hardly possible that this was the twentieth century, and that this was all real and not a dream of the scenes that Solomon and his people were accustomed to see "in the gates," to which he alluded when praising the virtuous woman: "Her husband is known in the gates, when he sitteth among the elders of the land." (Prov. xxxi, 23.)

"They hate him that rebuketh in the gate"; "They afflict the just, they take a bribe, and they turn aside the poor in the gate from their rights"; "Hate evil, and love the good, and establish judgment in the gate." (Amos v, 10, 12, 15.)

"They that sit in the gate speak against me." (Ps. lxix, 12.)

Ever since Moses stood in the gate of the camp and spoke to his erring people, the gates of the Far East have always been the favorite places for transacting business of all kinds and most frequented by the idle and the inquisitive. This Damascus Gate, as it stands to-day, dates back only to the beginning of the sixteenth century; an older structure was rebuilt by Solimân. Excavations prove that this gate is built on the foundations of an ancient one, for not only this but also a fragment of a wall built of great blocks of hewn stone were discovered here.

I felt that this was the very place where that gate stood, through which he was "brought as a lamb to the slaughter" to the place where "Jesus also, that he might sanctify the people with his own blood, suffered without the gate." (Heb. xiii, 12.)

Without this gate there is a green hill which many believe is "Golgotha, which is, being interpreted, The place of a skull," "called Calvary."

From a certain stand-point this hill, partly cut away by a quarry, resembles the form of a human skull.

Whether this or another place is the true spot where the Son of man was lifted up, as Moses lifted up the serpent in the wilderness, I will not dispute with any one; I will simply say that as I contemplated the momentous tragedy which ended when he said, "It is finished," it mattered little to me whether it occurred here or a few hundred yards away, because the transcendent truth entered my soul, although I could not understand it: "For God so loved the world, that he gave his only begotten Son, that whosoever believeth in him should not perish, but have everlasting life." (John iii, 16.)

"Surely he hath born our griefs, and carried our sorrows: yet we did esteem him stricken, smitten of God, and afflicted. But he was wounded for our transgressions, he was bruised for our iniquities: the chastisement of our peace was upon him: and with his stripes we are healed." (Isa. liii, 4, 5.)

He was crucified between two thieves as was foretold, "And he was numbered with the transgressors; and he bare the sins of many, and made intercession for the transgressors." (Isa. liii, 12.)

"Behold the Lamb of God which taketh away the sin of the world." (John i, 29.)

"And thou shalt call his name JESUS: for he shall save his people from their sins." (Matt. i, 21.)

"And Pilate wrote a title and put it on the cross. And the writing was, JESUS OF NAZARETH THE KING OF THE JEWS." (John xix, 19.)

"Neither is there salvation in any other: for there is none other name under heaven given among men, whereby we must be saved." (Acts iv, 12.)

"For even Christ our passover is sacrificed for us." (I Cor. v, 7.)

"Let us draw near with a true heart in full assurance of faith, having our hearts sprinkled from an evil conscience, and our bodies washed with pure water." (Heb. x, 22.)

Sacrifice for our sin we cannot offer, for He hath been sacrificed once for all, and He said, "It is finished"; but "a broken and a contrite heart, O God, thou wilt not despise."

"And behold, the veil of the temple was rent in twain from the top to the bottom." Now, through Jesus Christ, our high-priest, we may approach the mercy-seat, for "by his own blood he entered in once into the holy place, having obtained eternal redemption for us."

"Jesus saith unto him, I am the way, the truth, and the life: no man cometh unto the Father, but by me." "And I, if I be lifted up from the earth, will draw all men unto me."

"Now in the place where he was crucified there was a garden; and in the garden a new sepulchre, wherein was never man yet laid. There laid they Jesus therefore . . . for the sepulchre was nigh at hand." (John xix, 41, 42.)

"And he made his grave with the wicked, and with the rich in his death." (Isa. liii, 9.)

"When the even was come, there came a rich man of Arimathaea, named Joseph, who also himself was Jesus' disciple: He went to Pilate and begged the body of Jesus. Then Pilate commanded the body to be delivered. And when Joseph had taken the body, he wrapped it in a clean linen cloth, and laid it in his own new tomb, which he had hewn out in the rock: and he rolled a great stone to the door of the sepulchre and departed." (Matt. xxvii, 57, 58, 59, 60.)

Even to this day there is a small garden in one side of which there is a rocky cliff, in which there is an unfinished tomb; all of which is in keeping with the descriptions in the Bible. This tomb is called Gordon's Tomb, after the great English general who thought that this was the tomb where they laid Him.

As I have remarked before, nothing certain can be known about this and other places of sacred memory in Jerusalem until excavations can be made. But if this is not the one, it is an exact type of the stone tombs of that period. The chief priests and the Pharisees wishing to make sure that Christ would not rise again on the third day, after receiving permission from Pilate, went and made the sepulchre sure by sealing the stone and setting a watch.

Often have I read the different accounts of this stone in front of a tomb, but never did I have a clear idea of it until I came to the end of my camera crusade, when I found a tomb with "the stone rolled away."

"And when the sabbath was past, Mary Magdalene, and Mary the mother of James, and Salome had bought sweet spices, that they might come and anoint him. And very early in the morning the first day of the week, they came unto the sepulchre at the rising of the sun, And they said among themselves, Who shall roll us away the stone from the door of the sepulchre? And when they looked, they saw that the stone was rolled away: for it was very great." (Mark xvi.)

And when the women were afraid, the angel of the Lord said, "Fear not ye: for I know that ye seek Jesus, which was crucified. He is not here: for he is risen."

"But now is Christ risen from the dead and become the first-fruits of them that slept. For since by man came death, by man came also the resurrection of the dead. For as in Adam all die, even so in Christ shall all be made alive." (I Cor. xv.)

"But thanks be to God, which giveth us the victory through our Lord Jesus Christ." (I Cor. xv, 57.)

After showing himself to the women, our risen Lord went to Galilee as he had promised his disciples. There he met them, but they knew him not. "And it came to pass as he sat at meat with them, he took bread, and blessed it and brake, and gave to them." "And their eyes were opened, and they knew him." (Luke xxiv, 30, 31.)

May you ever know and remember him in the breaking of bread.

"For Jesus said unto them, I am the bread of life: he that cometh to me shall never hunger; and he that believeth on me shall never thirst." (John vi, 35.)

"Ho, every one that thirsteth, come ye to the waters, and he that hath no money, come ye, buy, and eat; yea, come, buy wine and milk without money and without price." (Isa. lv, 1.)

"Come unto me, all ye that labour and are heavy laden, and I will give you rest. Take my yoke upon you, and learn of me; for I am meek and lowly in heart: and ye shall find rest unto your souls. For my yoke is easy, and my burden is light." (Matt. xi, 28–30.)

"For the Lamb which is in the midst of the throne shall feed them, and shall lead them unto living fountains of waters: and God shall wipe away all tears from their eyes." (Rev. vii, 17.)

"Worthy is the Lamb that was slain to receive power, and riches, and wisdom, and strength, and honour, and glory, and blessing." (Rev. v, 12.)

And so I bear testimony to the things I found in the Holy Land, and to the truths I found in his Holy word, which "is a lamp unto my feet and a light unto my path."

"I will fear no evil," "For I know that my Redeemer liveth."

In the words of the beloved disciple John, I may humbly say:

"And he said unto me, Write: for these words are true and faithful."

PLATES AND TEXTS

PLATE II

JOPPA FROM THE SEA

II Chron. ii, 16.   And we will cut wood out of Lebanon, as much as thou shalt need; and we will bring it to thee in flotes by sea to Joppa; and thou shalt carry it up to Jerusalem.

Joshua xix, 46.
Ezra iii, 7.
Jonah i, 3.
Acts ix, 36, 43; xi, 5.

PLATE III

THE SEA FROM THE ROOF OF "ONE SIMON
A TANNER"

Acts ix, 43.   And it came to pass, that he tarried many days
in Joppa with one Simon a tanner.

Jonah i, 3.
Acts x, 6.

PLATE IV

A BREAD SELLER AT JOPPA

Gen. xviii, 5.   And I will fetch a morsel of bread.

Gen. xiv, 18; xxv, 34; xli, 54, 55; xliii, 25, 31, 32; xlv, **23.**
Ex. xvi, 4, 8, 12, 15, 32; xxiii, 25.
Lev. xxvi, 26.
Deut. viii.
Joshua ix, 5.
Judges vii, 13.
Ruth i, 6.
I Sam. ii, 36; xxii, 13; xxviii, 20, 22.
II Sam. vi, 19.
Prov. xii, 9, 11; xx, 13; xxii, 9; xxxi, 27.
Eccl. ix, 11.
Isaiah xxxiii, 16; lv, 2.
Matt. iv, 3, 4; vi, 11; vii, 9; xxvi, 26.
Mark viii, 14.
Luke iv, 4; xxiv, 35.
John vi, 7–32–35, 50, 51.

PLATE V

PLAIN OF SHARON FROM THE TOWER OF RAMLEH

Isaiah lxv,
10.

And Sharon shall be a fold of flocks, and the valley of Achor a place for herds to lie down in, for my people that have sought me.

I Chron. v, 16; xxvii, 29; viii, 12.
Song Sol. ii, 1.
Isaiah xxxiii, 9; xxxv, 2.

PLATE VI

THE ROSES OF SHARON

Song Sol. ii.   I am the rose of Sharon and the lily of the valley.

Song Sol. vi, 3; v, 13.
Hosea xiv, 5.
Matt. vi, 28, 29.

PLATE VII

PLOUGHING

Deut. xxii, 10. Thou shalt not plough with an ox and an ass together.

I Sam. xiii, 19; xiv, 14.
Job iv, 8; i, 14.
Prov. xx, 4.
Isaiah xxviii, 24.
Acts ix, 5.
I Cor. ix, 10.
II Cor. vi, 14, 15, 16.

PLATE VIII

THE VALLEY OF ESHCOL

Num. xxxii,   They went up into the valley of Eshcol.
9.

Num. xiii, 17, 23, 24.

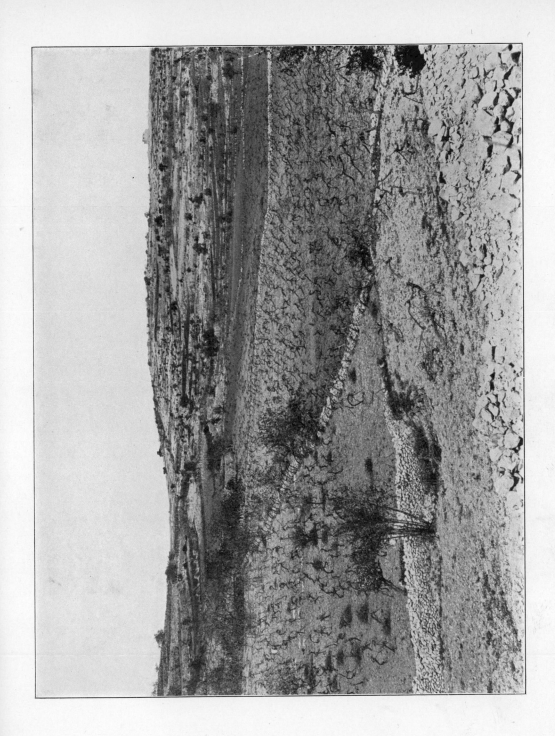

PLATE IX

ABRAHAM'S OAK

Gen. xviii, 4.   And rest yourselves under the oak.

Gen. xiii, 18; xxiii, 17, 18.

PLATE X

HEBRON—THE POOL AND THE MOSQUE

Gen. xxiii, 2.   And Sarah died in Kirjath-arba; the same is
Hebron in the land of Canaan.

Gen. xii, 18; xxiii, 2, 9, 17, 20; xxxv, 27.
Num. xiii, 22.
Joshua x, 36; xiv, 13; xxi, 13; xv, 13.
II Sam. ii, 1, 11, 27, 35; iii, 2; iv, 12; v, 1; xv, 10.
I Chron. xi, 1–3; xii, 38; xxix, 27.

PLATE XI

SOLOMON'S POOL

II Kings xviii, 17.
Isaiah vii, 3; xxxvi, 2.
Neh. ii, 14.

PLATE XII

THE VILLAGE OF THE SHEPHERDS

Jer. xxiii, 4.
Isaiah xl, 11.
Luke ii, 8.

PLATE XIII

SHEPHERDS WATCHING THEIR FLOCKS

Jer. xxiii, 4.   And I will set up shepherds over them which
shall feed them.

Psalm xxiii, 2.
Jer. xxxi, 28.
Luke ii, 8.

PLATE XIV

THE CITY OF DAVID WHICH IS CALLED BETHLEHEM

Luke ii, 4.   And Joseph also went up from Galilee out of the city of Nazareth unto Judæa; into the city of David which is called Bethlehem.

Gen. xlix, 10.
Ex. xiii, 2.
Num. xxiv, 17.
Deut. xviii, 16.
II Sam. xxiii, 15.
I Chron. xi, 17.
Psalm ii, 7; cxviii, 22; cxxxii, 11.
Isaiah vii, 14; xi, 1; lx, 1–3; lxxii, 10–12.
Micah v, 2.
Zech. iii, 8; vi, 12.
Matt. ii, 1–8; viii, 29; xiv, 33; xxvi, 63; xxvii, 43, 54.
Luke i, 35; iv, 41; xxii, 70.
John i, 14, 34; iii, 16, 18; vi, 69; ix, 35–37; xx, 31; vii, 42.

PLATE XV

THE MANGER IN THE CHURCH OF THE NATIVITY

Matt. ii, 9.   When they heard the king, they departed; and, lo, the star which they saw in the east went before them till it came and stood where the young child was.

Luke ii, 7, 12, 16.

PLATE XVI

THE FIELDS OF BOAZ

Luke iii, 32.
Ruth, ii.

PLATE XVII

RUTH AND BOAZ

Lev. xix, 9, 10; xxiii, 22.
Deut. xxiv, 19.
Ruth ii.

PLATE XVIII

A THRESHING FLOOR

Gen. l, 10.   And they came to the threshing floor of Atad.
Lev. xxvi, 5; xxv. 19.
Num. xv, 20.
Deut. xv, 14.
Ruth iii, 2.
II Sam. xxiv, 18–22.
I Chron. xxi, 21–26.
II Chron. iii, 1.
Isaiah xxi, 10; xxviii, 28.
Joel ii, 24.
Micah iv, 11–13.
Matt. iii, 12.

PLATE XIX

SHEPHERDS LEADING THEIR FLOCKS

Jer. xxiii, 4.   And I will set up shepherds over them which
shall feed them.

Psalm xxiii, 1.
Isaiah xl, 11.
Ezek. xxxiv, 6–23.
John x, 4, 5, 7–16.
Heb. xiii, 20.
I Peter ii, 25; v, 4.
Rev. vii, 17.

PLATE XX

SHEPHERD'S PIPES, SLING, AND SCRIP

I Sam. xvii, 40-54; x, 5; xxv, 29.
I Kings i, 40.
II Kings iv, 25.
II Chron. xxvi, 14.
Isaiah v, 12; xxx, 29.
Jer. xlviii, 36.
Prov. xxvi, 8.
Matt. xi, 17; x, 10.
Luke ix, 3; x, 4; xxii, 35, 36.
I Cor. xiv, 7.
Rev. xviii, 22.

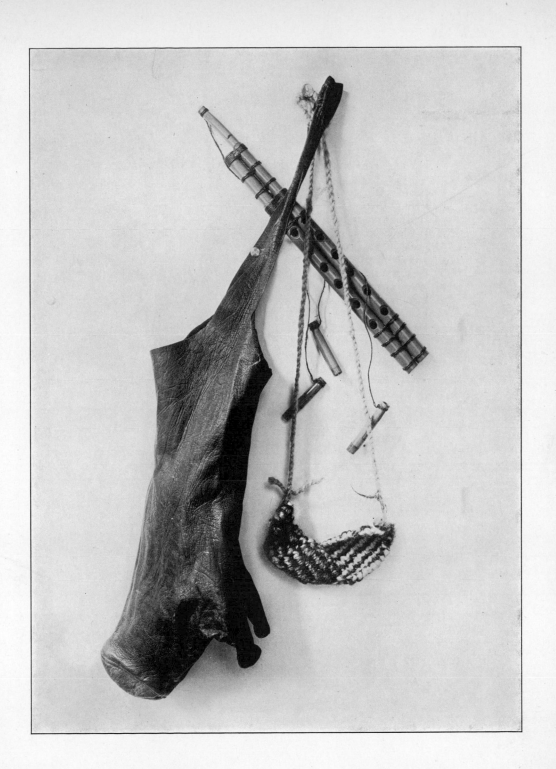

PLATE XXI

THE BROOK KIDRON AT MARSABA

II Sam. xv, 23.
John xviii, 1.

PLATE XXII

THE WILDERNESS OF THE SCAPEGOAT

Lev. xvi, 22.   And the goat shall bear upon him all their iniquities into a land not inhabited: and he shall let go the goat in the wilderness.

Lev. xvi, 20+.
I Sam. xxii, 1; xxiii, 14.

Psalms lxiii   David's prayers in the wilderness.
and clxii.

Isaiah xl, 3; liii, 6.
Matt. iii, 1–3; xi, 7.
Mark i, 3.
Luke iii, 4; xv, 4.
John i, 23.

PLATE XXIII

THE SALT OR THE DEAD SEA

Gen. xiv, 3.   The vale of Siddim which is the salt sea.

Gen. xiv, 1–3; xviii, 16; xix, 28.
Num. xxxiv, 12.
Deut. iii, 17; xxix, 23.
Joshua xii, 3; xv, 2; xviii, 19.
Isaiah i, 9; iii, 9; xiii, 19.
Jer. iv, 26, 27; xxiii, 14; l, 40.
Lam. iv, 6.
Ezek. xvi, 46–55.
Amos iv, 11.
Zeph. ii, 9.
Matt. x, 15; xi, 24.
Mark vi, 11.
Luke x, 12; xvii, 29.
Rom. ix, 29.
II Peter ii, 6
Jude, 7.

PLATE XXIV

THE SHORE OF THE DEAD SEA

Jer. l, 40.   As God overthrew Sodom and Gomorrah and
the neighbor cities thereof saith the Lord; so
shall no man abide there, neither shall any son
of man dwell therein.

Gen. xiii, 10; xviii, 20 + xix, 24, 28.
Deut. xxxii, 32.
Isaiah i, 9.
Jer. xxiii, 14; xlix, 18.
Amos iv, 11.
Zeph. ii, 9.
II Peter ii, 6.

PLATE XXV

THE JORDAN FORD

Matt. iii, 6.   And were baptized of him in Jordan, confessing
their sins.

Joshua iii, 16.
Matt. iii, 13.
Mark i, 5–11.
Luke iii, 21–38.

PLATE XXVI

LOOKING UP THE JORDAN

Joshua xxii. 25. The Lord hath made Jordan a border between us and you.

Joshua iii, 14–17.
II Sam. xvii, 22; xix, 15.
II Kings ii, 13; v, 10.
I Chron. xii, 15; xix, 17.
Isaiah xlviii, 18.
Ezek. xlvii, 5–18.

PLATE XXVII

ELISHA'S SPRING NEAR JERICHO

II Kings ii, 19–22.
Psalm xlii, 1.
Isaiah xliv, 3; xlvi, 4.
John vi, 35.
Rev. xxi, 6; xxii, 1, 17.

PLATE XXVIII

THE MOUNT OF TEMPTATION

Matt. iv, 8.   Again the devil taketh him up into an exceeding
              high mountain.

Luke iv, 5.
Mark i, 13.

PLATE XXIX

THE JERICHO ROAD AND THE SAMARITAN INN

Luke x,   A certain Samaritan went to him and bound up
30–37.   his wounds . . . and brought him to an inn.

PLATE XXX

THE BROOK CHERITH

I Kings   Hide thyself by the brook Cherith.
   xvii, 3.

I Kings xviii.

PLATE XXXI

THE APOSTLES' SPRING ON THE JERICHO ROAD

PLATE XXXII

WILDERNESS OF JUDÆA FROM JERICHO ROAD

Jer. xxxiii, 10, 12, 13.
Matt. xi, 7; iii, 1.
Luke vii, 24; ix, 51; xv, 4.
II Cor. xi, 26.

PLATE XXXIII

THE SHADOW OF A GREAT ROCK

Isaiah xxxii, 2.   The shadow of a great rock.

Psalms xci, 1; xvii, 8; xxxvi, 7; lvii, 1; lxi, 2, 3, 4; lxiii, 7; xci, 4.
Isaiah iv, 6; xxv, 4.
Ruth ii, 12.

PLATE XXXIV

BETHANY

Matt. xxi, 17.	He left them and went out of the city into Bethany and he lodged there.

Matt. xxvi, 6–13.
Mark xi, 12; xiv, 3; xvi, 19.
Luke xix, 29; xxiv, 50, 51.
John xi, 1–46; xii, 1–15.

RUIN OF THE SUPPOSED HOUSE OF MARY
AND MARTHA

Luke x, 38–42.
John xi, 1–46.

PLATE XXXVI

TWO WOMEN GRINDING

Matt. xxiv, 41.   Two women shall be grinding at the mill.

Matt. xviii, 6.
Mark ix, 42.
Luke xvii, 2, 35.
Ex. xi, 5.
Judges ix, 53; xvi, 21.
Isaiah xlvii, 2.

PLATE XXXVII

THE MOUNT OF OLIVES

Matt. xxvi, 30.   They went out into the Mount of Olives.

Matt. xxi, 1; xxiv, 3.
Mark xi, 1; xiii, 3; xiv, 26.
Luke xix, 37; xxii, 39; xxi, 37.
Zech. xiv, 4.
Ezek. xi, 23.

PLATE XXXVIII

NORTH–EAST CORNER OF JERUSALEM, MIZPAH
IN THE BACKGROUND

I Sam. vii, 5–12.
I Kings xv, 22.
II Kings xxv, 22–26.
Joshua xviii, 26.
Judges x, 17; xi, 11, 29.
Gen. xxxi, 49.
Jer. xl, 10; xli, 3.
Neh. iii, 7.
Hosea v, 1.

PLATE XXXIX

BETHEL

Gen. xxviii,   And he called the name of that place Bethel.
  19.

Gen. xxviii, 10–22; xxxv, 1–15; xxxi, 13.
Joshua xviii, 13, 22.
Judges i, 22, 23, 26.
I Kings xii, 29.
II Kings x, 29.
Jer. vii, 11.
Amos iii, 14; iv, 4; v, 5, 6; vii, 13.

PLATE XL

A JUDÆAN HIGHWAY

Matt. xxii, 9.
Luke xiv, 23.
Mark x, 46.

Go ye therefore into the highways.

PLATE XLI

LOOKING NORTH TOWARD SHILOH

Joshua xviii,   And the whole congregation of the children of
   1.   Israel assembled together at Shiloh, and set up
the tabernacle of the congregation there.

Deut. xii, 5, 11, 14.
Joshua xviii, 8; xix, 51; xxii, 9.
Judges xviii, 31; xxi, 12, 19, 21.
I Sam. i, 3, 9, 24; ii, 14; iii, 1–21; iv, 3–22; v; vi; vii.
I Kings ii, 27; xiv, 2.
Psalm lxxviii, 60.
Jer. vii, 12; xxvi, 6; xli, 5.

PLATE XLII

SHECHEM AND MOUNT GERIZIM

Joshua
xxiv, 1.

And Joshua gathered all the tribes of Israel to Shechem.

Gen. xii, 6; xxxiii, 18; xxxvii, 12, 13, 14.
Joshua xx, 7; xxi, 21; xxiv, 1, 32.
Judges ix, 1, 7, 20, 23, 41, 57.
I Kings xii, 1, 25.
Jer. vii, 12, 14; xxvi; xli, 5.

PLATE XLIII

THE OLD CODEX AT SHECHEM

Joshua viii, 34.　　And afterward he read all the words of the law, the blessings and the cursings, according to all that is written in the book of the law.

Deut. xvii, 18.
Joshua viii, 34.
II Kings xxii, 8, 13.
Mark xii, 10.
Luke xxiv, 27; iv, 17-21.
John v, 39, 46; vii, 42, 52.

PLATE XLIV

FROM MOUNT EBAL OVER SYCHAR, JACOB'S WELL, AND MOUNT GERIZIM

Gen. xxxiii, 19.
Deut. xi, 29; xxvii, 12.
Joshua viii, 33.
Judges ix, 7.

PLATE XLV

RUINS OVER THE SITE OF JACOB'S WELL

PLATE XLVI

SYCHAR, JACOB'S WELL, AND MOUNT GERIZIM

John iv, 6.   Now Jacob's well was there.

John iv, 3–26.
Isaiah xii, 3.
Jer. ii, 13.
Rev. xxi, 6.

PLATE XLVII

THE MIDST OF SAMARIA

Luke xvii,
11.

Isaiah xxviii,
1–4.

John iv, 4.

Acts viii, 1.

And it came to pass as he went to Jerusalem
that he passed through the midst of Samaria.

PLATE XLVIII

THE CITY OF SAMARIA (SEBASTE)

I Kings xvi,   And he bought the hill Samaria of Shemer . . .
24.   and called the name of the city . . . Samaria.

I Kings xvi, 32; xxii, 37; xx, 1.
II Kings vi, 24, 25; vii, 1.
Matt. ii, 12, 15, 16; xiv, 1.
Mark viii, 15; vi, 14–26.
Luke iii, 1, 19; ix, 7.
Acts viii, 5.

PLATE XLIX

HEROD'S COLUMNS AT SAMARIA, OR SEBASTE

PLATE L

THE PLAIN OF JEZREEL

I Sam.   And Ahab rode and went to Jezreel.
   xxix, 1.

Judges i, 27.
II Sam. ii, 9.
I Kings xviii, 44, 45, 46; xxi, 1.
II Kings viii, 29; ix, 10–37; x, 1–11; xxiii, 29, 30.
Joshua xvii, 11, 16.
II Chron. xxxv, 22.

PLATE LI

PLOUGHING IN THE PLAIN OF JEZREEL

I Sam. xiv,   A yoke of oxen might plough.
  14.

Deut. xxii, 10.
Job iv, 8; i, 14.
Prov. xx, 1.
Isaiah xxviii, 24.
Luke ix, 62.
Acts ix, 5; v, ci; viii, G.
I Cor. ix, 10.
II Cor. vi, 14, 15, 16.

PLATE LII

A JORDAN FORD

II Kings v, 14.   Then he went down and dipped himself seven times in Jordan.

II Kings v, whole chapter.
Judges vii, 24.
Luke iv, 27.
John i, 28; x, 40.

PLATE LIII

MOUNT TABOR FROM MOUNT CARMEL

Judges iv, 6, 12–23; viii, 18.
I Sam. x, 3; xxv, 2.
I Kings xviii, 17–46.
Psalm lxxxix, 12.
Cant. vii, 5.
Jer. xlvi, 18.

PLATE LIV

NAZARETH FROM THE DAMASCUS ROAD

Luke iv, 16. And he came to Nazareth where he had been
brought up . . .

Judges xiii, 5.
I Sam. i, 11.
Matt. ii, 23; xxi, 11.
Mark i, 24; x, 47; xiv, 67.
Luke i, 26; ii, 51; iv, 16, 34: xviii, 37; xxiv, 19.
John i, 45; xviii, 5, 7; xix, 19.
Acts ii, 22; iii, 6; iv, 10; vi, 14; xxii, 8.

PLATE LV

MARY'S WELL AT NAZARETH

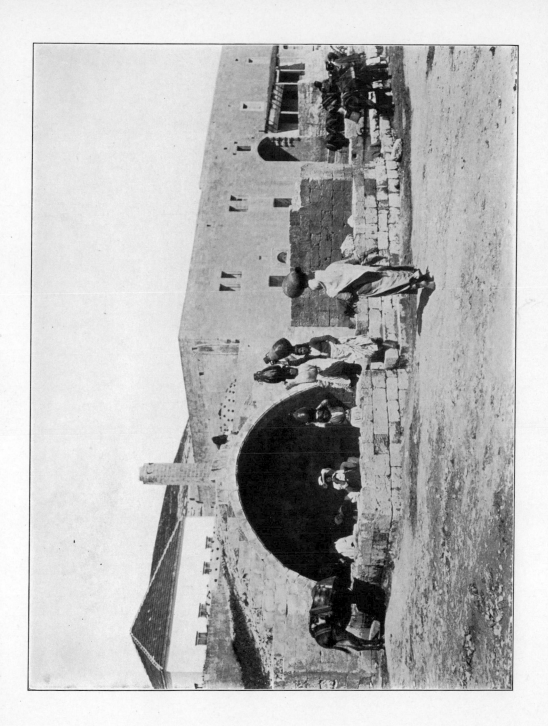

PLATE LVI

NAZARETH TOWARD MOUNT CARMEL

PLATE LVII

CANA OF GALILEE

John ii, 1.   And the third day there was a marriage in Cana
of Galilee.

John ii, 1–11; iv, 46; xxi, 2.
Joshua xix, 28.

PLATE LVIII

MOUNT OF THE BEATITUDES

Matt. v, 1.　　And seeing a multitude he went up into a
mountain.

Matt. v; vi; vii.

PLATE LIX

THE SEA OF GALILEE

John vi, 1.   After these things Jesus went over the Sea of Galilee, which is the Sea of Tiberias.

John xxi, 1.
Matt. viii, 23–27; xiv, 34.
Mark iv, 36–41; v, 1; vi, 47–51.
Luke v, 1.

PLATE LX

FISHERMEN CASTING THEIR NETS

Matt.iv,18.   And Jesus walking by the Sea of Galilee saw two brethren, Simon called Peter, and Andrew his brother, casting a net into the sea : for they were fishers.

Matt. iv, 18, 19, 20.
Mark i, 16, 17.
Luke v, 1-11.
John xxi.

PLATE LXI

OVER THE SEA TOWARD CAPERNAUM

John vi, 17.   Over the sea toward Capernaum.

Matt. iv, 13; viii, 5; ix, 1; xi, 23; xvii, 24.
Mark ii, 1.
Luke iv, 23, 31; vii, 1; viii, 22–25; x, 15.
John ii, 12; vi, 17, 24, 59.

PLATE LXII

WHERE THE JORDAN ENTERS THE SEA OF GALILEE

Matt. xiv, 13 ff.
Mark vi, 34 ff.
Luke ix, 10 ff.
John vi ff.

PLATE LXIII

UPPER JORDAN VALLEY

Psalm xxiii, 2.
Ezek. xxxiv, 14.

PLATE LXIV

BEDOUIN TENTS

Judges vi, 5.   For they come up with their cattle and their tents.

Gen. iv, 20.

PLATE LXV

THE WATERS OF MEROM AND MOUNT HERMON

Joshua xi, 5–7

PLATE LXVI

STILL WATERS

Psalm
xxiii, 2.

He leadeth me beside the still waters.

Ezek. xxxiv, 11–15.
Matt. xxv, 32.
Rev. vii, 17.

PLATE LXVII

ROMAN BRIDGE OVER THE JORDAN

Old Damascus Road near Dan

PLATE LXVIII

AN OAK TREE

I Kings
xiii, 14.

And went after the man of God, and found him sitting under an oak.

Gen. xxxv, 4, 8.
Joshua xxiv, 26.
II Sam. xviii, 9 ff.
I Kings xiii, 14.
I Chron. x, 12.
Isaiah xliv, 14.
Ezek. xxvii, 6.
Hosea iv, 13.

PLATE LXIX

OLD ROMAN BRIDGE NEAR DAN
(CÆSAREA PHILIPPI)

Gen. xiv, 14.
Deut. xxxiv, 1.
Judges xviii, 29, 30.

PLATE LXX

THE SOURCE OF THE JORDAN

Joshua   Baal-gad under Mount Hermon.
    xiii, 5.

Joshua xi, 17; xii, 7.
Judges iii, 3.
Matt. xvi, 13-16.
Mark viii, 27-29.

PLATE LXXI

DAMASCUS

Gen. xv, 2. And Abram said, Lord God, what wilt thou give
me, seeing I go childless, and the steward of my
house is this Eliezer of Damascus?

II Sam. viii, 6.
I Kings xi, 23–35.
II Kings v, 12; viii, 7; xiv, 28; xvi, 9–12.
Isaiah vii, 8; viii, 4; xvii, 1–3.
Ezek. xxvii, 18.
Amos i, 3; v, 27.
Acts ix, 1–27; xxii, 5–30; xxvi, 12.
II Cor. xi, 32, 33.
Gal. i, 17.

PLATE LXXII

SNOWY PEAKS OF MOUNT HERMON

Psalm   He giveth snow like wool.
  cxlvii, 16.

Psalm li, 7; lxxxix, 12; cxxxiii, 3.
Deut. iii, 8, 9; iv, 48.
Joshua xiii, 5, 11.
Song of Sol. iv, 8.
Prov. xxv, 13.
Isaiah i, 18; lv, 10.
Matt. xvii, 1–9.
Mark ix, 2–10.
Luke ix, 28–36.

PLATE LXXIII

MOUNT LEBANON

Deut. iii, 25.   I pray thee let me go over and see the good land that is beyond Jordan, that goodly mountain and Lebanon.

Judges iii, 3.
I Kings v, 14; vii, 2.
II Kings xiv, 9.
II Chron. ii, 8.
Psalm xxix, 5, 6; lxxii, 16; xcii, 12.
Song of Sol. iii, 9.
Isaiah x, 32; xxix, 17; xxxv, 2; xxxvii, 24; lx, 13; xl, 16.
Jer. xviii, 14; xxii, 6.
Zech. x, 10.
Ezek. xxvii. 5.

PLATE LXXIV

THE HEART OF JERUSALEM FROM THE MOUNT OF OLIVES

Psalm
cxxii, 3.
Jerusalem is builded as a city that is compact together.

Joshua xviii, 28.
II Sam. v, 5, 7.
I Kings iii, 1; xi, 13.
II Kings xxiii, 27.
Neh. xi, 1.
Psalm xlviii; cxvi, 19.
Isaiah lii.
Mal. iii, 4.
Matt. xvi, 21; xxiii, 37–39.
Luke ii, 22; xiii, 34, 35; xxi, 20; xxiv, 47–49.
John iv, 20; xii, 12.
Acts xxi, 31.

PLATE LXXV

THE MOSQUE OF OMAR ON THE SITE OF THE TEMPLE OF JERUSALEM

Psalm lxvii, 29.
I Kings vi.
II Chron. iii; iv; v.

PLATE LXXVI

THE DOME OF THE ROCK

I Kings vi, 16; viii, 6–30.
II Chron. ii, 1–4; v, 7–14.
Ezek. xliii, 12.
Joel iii, 17.
Zech. viii, 3.
Isaiah ii, 2, 3.

PLATE LXXVII

THE CHURCH OF THE HOLY SEPULCHRE

*Greek ceremony "washing of feet" at the door of the church
on Easter Sunday*

PLATE LXXVIII

THE THRONG OF PILGRIMS AND OTHERS

At the door of the Church of the Holy Sepulchre,
Easter morning

PLATE LXXIX

AN OLD HOUSE WITH AN UPPER CHAMBER

Mark xiv,
15.

And he will show you a large upper room furnished and prepared: there make ready for us.

Matt. xxvi, 18–20.
Luke xxii, 12.
Acts i, 13.

Luke ii, 7,
12, 16.

Beneath the upper chamber there was a typical Syrian manger.

PLATE LXXX

COINS USED IN PALESTINE DURING THE TIME OF OUR LORD

No. 1. A silver denarius, or penny, of Tiberius, the tribute money payable by the Jews to the Roman emperor. Worth about seventeen cents, American money.

No. 2. A silver denarius, or penny, of Augustus, also worth $0.17.

No. 3. A silver shekel of Jerusalem, worth about $0.54, coined by Simon Maccabæus about 140 B. C.

The shekel in the Old Testament was an Assyrian weight of 258 grains, while this silver shekel of Jerusalem weighs 220 grains. On the obverse side is a chalice or cup of Manna, on the reverse a triple lily or Aaron's budding rod and the inscription "Jerusalem the holy."

Nos. 4 and 5 are "pieces of silver," so often mentioned, and are worth about $0.56½. "Thirty pieces of silver" were worth $16.96, the legal value of a slave if he were killed by a beast. Judas betrayed our Lord for $16.96.

"Pieces of silver" in the Old Testament were not these coins, but weights of silver shaped like a lamb.

These two coins date from 126 B. C. to 57 A. D.

REFERENCES TO THE PENNY

Matt. xviii, 28; xx, 2, 9; xxii, 19–21.
Mark vi, 37; xii, 15–17; xiv, 5.
Luke vii, 41; x, 35.
John xii, 5; vi, 7.
Rev. vi, 6.

REFERENCES TO "PIECES OF SILVER"

Gen. xx, 16; xxxiii, 19; xxxvii, 28; xlv, 22.
Judges ix, 4; xvi, 5.
II Kings vi, 25.
Zech. xi, 12, 13.
Matt. xxvi, 15; xxvii, 9.
Luke xv, 8.
Acts xix, 19.

REFERENCES TO THE SHEKEL

Gen. xxiii, 15, 16.
Ex. xxi, 32; xxx, 13, 15; xxxvii, 24.
Lev. xxvii, 3–16, 25; v, 15.
Num. iii, 47; Ezek. iv, 10; xlv, 12; Joshua vii, 21.
Judges viii, 26; xvii, 2, 3, 10.
I Sam. ix, 8. II Sam. xiv, 26. II Kings vii, 1, 16, 18; xv, 20.
I Chron. xxi, 25. Neh. v, 15; x, 32.
Jer. xxxii, 9. Amos viii, 5.

(Through the courtesy of the American Numismatic Society I was permitted to photograph these fine specimens of coins now in their museum in New York City.)

PLATE LXXXI

THE POOL OF BETHESDA

John v, 2–9.   A pool which is called Bethesda.

PLATE LXXXII

AN OLD STREET, JERUSALEM

Song of Sol. iii, 2.

PLATE LXXXIII

THE WAILING PLACE OF THE JEWS, JERUSALEM

Isaiah lix, 10, 11.

We grope for the wall like the blind, and we grope as if we had no eyes: we roar all like bears, and mourn sore like doves: we look for judgment, but there is none; for salvation, but it is far off from us.

Isaiah xliv, 18; lix, 1. 2.
Deut. iv, 25–40.

PLATE LXXXIV

WEST WALL OF JERUSALEM

Psalm xlviii.   Mark ye well her bulwarks.
  12–14.

Psalm lxi, 3.
Song of Sol. iv, 4.
II Chron. xiv, 7; xxxii, 5.

PLATE LXXXV

POOL OF GIHON

| II Chron. xxxii, 30. | This same Hezekiah also stopped the upper watercourse of Gihon. |

I Kings i, 33.
Isaiah xxii, 9–11.

PLATE LXXXVI

SOUTH-EASTERN SLOPE OF MOUNT ZION

*Mount of Olives in the background, the village of Siloam on the right,
and the Valley of Hinnom in the foreground.*

II Sam. v, 7.
I Kings viii, 1.
Psalm xlviii; cxxxii, 13.

PLATE LXXXVII

THE VALLEY OF HINNOM, GEHENNA

Joshua xv, 8.
II Kings xxiii, 10.
II Chron. xxviii, 3; xxxiii, 6.
Jer. xix, 2–6; xxxii, 35.
Matt. xxvi, 3.

PLATE LXXXVIII

THE POOL OF SILOAM

Neh. iii, 15.
John ix, whole chapter.

PLATE LXXXIX

THE TYROPŒAN VALLEY

The Mosque of Aksa appearing above the city wall.

PLATE XC

THE KING'S DALE AND JOB'S WELL

*Kidron Valley on the left, Job's Well in the centre, Valley of
Hinnom on the right.*

II Sam. xv, 23; xvii, 17–19.
Joshua xv, 7.
I Kings i, 9.

PLATE XCI

SOUTH–EAST CORNER OF THE TEMPLE WALL, LOOKING NORTH

Kidron Valley and the village of Siloam.

II Sam. xv, 23.
Luke xiii, 4.

PLATE XCII

THE SPRING OF MARY, OR THE VIRGIN'S WELL

Joshua ix, 4, 13, 21.
Matt. ix, 17.
Mark ii, 22.
Luke v, 37, 38.

PLATE XCIII

THE VALLEY OF JEHOSHAPHAT, LOOKING UP KIDRON VALLEY

Joel iii, 2, 12.   Let the heathen be wakened, and come up to the valley of Jehoshaphat: for there will I sit to judge all the heathen round about.

II Sam. xv, 23.

PLATE XCV

THE GARDEN OF GETHSEMANE AND THE CITY
WALL OF JERUSALEM

John xviii, 1.

PLATE XCVI

THE GARDEN OF GETHSEMANE

Matt. xxvi, 36.
Mark xiv, 32.
Luke xxii, 39.
John xviii, 1.

PLATE XCVII

THE DAMASCUS GATE

Heb. xiii,
12.

Wherefore Jesus also, that he might sanctify the people with his own blood, suffered without the gate.

Micah i, 9.
Amos v, 10, 12, 15.
Prov. xxxi, 23.
Psalm lxix, 12.

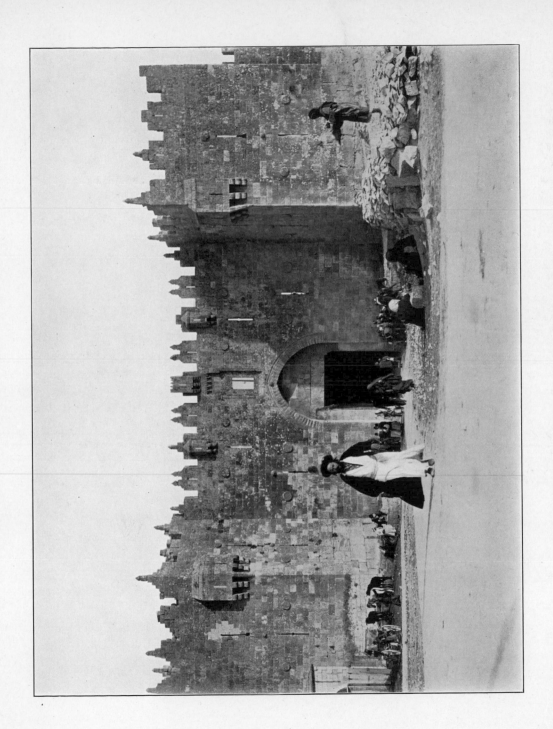

PLATE XCVIII

A GREEN HILL WITHOUT A CITY WALL

Matt. xxvii, 33.   A place called Golgotha, that is to say, a place of a skull.

Matt. xxvii, 34–53.
Mark 22–38.
Luke xxiii, 33–49.
John i, 29; iii, 16; xii, 32; xix, 16–24.
I Cor. v, 7.
Heb. xiii, 12.
Psalm lxix, 16–21.
Isaiah liii, whole chapter.
Rev. xxi, 6.

PLATE XCIX

GORDON'S TOMB

Isaiah liii,　　And he made his grave with the wicked, and
　9.　　　　with the rich in his death.

Matt. xxviii, 57–60.
Mark xv, 43–47.
Luke xxiii, 50–56.
John xix, 38–42.

PLATE C

THE STONE ROLLED AWAY

Luke xxiv, 2.   And they found the stone rolled away from the sepulchre.

Psalm xvi, 10.
Matt. xxviii, 2.
Mark xvi, 4.
John ii, 19–22; vi, 39, 40, 44, 54; xi, 25; xx, 1.
Acts xxvi, 23; ii, 23–32; xxvi, 18.
Rom. iv, 26; vi, 4–10.
I Cor. xv, 20–26; vi, 14.
II Cor. iv, 14–18.
James v, 15.
Rev. xxi, 5, 6; xxii, whole chapter